C000180734

A journal of nature & story

**Get in touch**

info@elementumjournal.com

**Elementum Journal**

The Grain Loft, South Street,
Sherborne, Dorset
DT9 3LU, United Kingdom

**Connect**

Twitter @elementumjournl
Instagram @elementumjournal
Facebook @elementumjournal

**Buy or subscribe online**

www.elementumjournal.com/shop

**Become a stockist**

If you would like to stock
*Elementum*, please contact
trade@elementumjournal.com

**Cover image**

*Pahoehoe Lava from Kalapana,
Hawaiʻi* by Leigh Hilbert

**Argyll – the Enduring Heartland**

From *Argyll: The Enduring Heartland* by
Marion Campbell (3rd ed., 2011) reprinted
with permission of House of Lochar.

**Ocean Paths**

Images courtesy of the Scientific Visualization
Studio, Goddard Space Flight Center,
North American Space Agency.

**From the Heart of the Tree**

The publisher and author would like to acknowledge
the generous assistance and guidance from kuʻualoha
hoʻomanawanui, Professor of Hawaiian Literature, University
of Hawaiʻi at Manoa, in the developmet of this piece.

The author is further indebted to several sources, including
the volumes *Legends of Maui* by W.D. Westervelt (1910) (in
particular, for the Polynesian chant), *Myths and Legends of the
Polynesians* by Johannes C. Andersen (1928) and *Handbook
of Polynesian Mythology* by Robert D. Craig (2004).

**Talismans and Tombstones**

Quotes reproduced from *The Irish Cottage: History,
Culture and Design* by Marion McGarry (2017).

For the hearth keepers and the fire starters.

ISBN 978-0-9956740-3-5   ISSN 2398-6301

A CIP record for this book is available from the British Library.

*Elementum Journal* is a biannual publication.

Printed in the UK on FSC-certified paper.

Contents copyright 2019 Elementum Journal

All rights reserved. No part of this publication may be reproduced without permission from the publishers. The views expressed in *Elementum Journal* are
not necessarily those of the contributors, editors or publishers. *Elementum Journal* reserves the right to edit contents prior to publication.

# HEARTH

EDITION FIVE

ELEMENTUM

## CONTRIBUTORS

### WRITERS

Sara Baume

Zetta Bear

Marion Campbell

Monica Coyne

Jim Crumley

Nicola Davies

Wyl Menmuir

Laura Morgan

Stephen Moss

Eleanor Parker

Helen Scales

Colin Taylor

Annie Worsley

Raynor Winn

### PHOTOGRAPHERS & ARTISTS

Georgie Bennett

Lucy Eldridge

Neil Gower

Leigh Hilbert

Catherine Hyde

Jenny McLaren

Justine Osborne

Magi Sinclair

### EDITORS

Hazel Bird

Sophia Gallia

Susannah Marriott

Kym Martindale

### EDITORIAL & CREATIVE DIRECTION

Jay Armstrong

### CREATIVE & MARKETING

Gill Crew

Mike Hayes

Sam McArthur

Leigh Peregrine

Helen Stickland

### ACCOUNTS & DEVELOPMENT

Scott Armstrong

Kate Hillam

Alison Nurton

## FOREWORD

Among my most treasured possessions are three misshapen grey stones. Together they fit easily in the palm of my hand and weigh less than you might expect. Their roughened surface is crazed with tiny cracks. Nondescript. You would be forgiven for thinking I had found them on a building site. However, as my friend Jane told me as she picked them out of the sandy earth, they are Neolithic cooking stones, which would have been baked in a simple fire pit and most probably used to heat water. Holding them, I have a familiar thrill of encounter and see in my mind's eye a thread spooling back thousands of years to a community living on what is now Stanpit Marsh in Dorset, perhaps back to the mother who last held them, working by a fire, doing what needed to be done for her own.

'Hearth', the theme that binds this edition together, is our most domesticated focus yet, but the contributions are far from tame. All too often, the human world is perceived as distinct from, or even above, the natural world. Settlement has been a fundamental means of human advancement, but at the same time it is largely responsible for this disconnection and the resulting ecological impact. Living lightly on the earth, with humility, respect and responsibility, is the undercurrent that runs through each feature. From taming our wildness by learning from the animals we invite across our threshold, to leaning in to the land to fathom what nature has to tell us, or looking back at the earth from sky or ocean to consider a planet without borders – each writer and artist invites the reader to a different way of seeing and hearing.

In preparing this edition, I had the privilege of spending time with contributor artist-blacksmith Monica Coyne. She is fully aware of the role her craft has played in human development and the resources it has consumed. In asking how we can better fit into the world, she writes:

> We have been here a while. We have been drawing pictures and making sculptures for more than fifty thousand years. That gives us occupancy of this place. We are supposed to be here. The cement on the city sidewalk is just as natural as the haystack of wooden sticks that makes up the woodrats' nest behind my garden shed. … Everything here on Earth is made from the same building blocks. … We are part of a closed system. These building blocks can help us to see a way forward. Listen.

Now that this edition is complete, I see more clearly that we need a multitude of voices and perspectives, a collaboration of different viewpoints, cultures and experiences to understand our own more fully. Earth is a shared home to every living thing and only by listening, looking and learning will we find a better way forward.

On a different scale, *Elementum* has recently moved to a beautiful honeyed sandstone building that was once a grain store. Here we have opened a gallery where we can bring together the work of our contributors, alongside that of other artists and writers, and invite our readers to join us for courses and talks. It is a daunting prospect, but it feels as if the journal has found a home. We now have a place to gather, grow and learn – the perfect hearth.

**Jay Armstrong**
Editor

# CONTENTS

# THE FIRE PIT

## STONE-HENGED AND STONE-LINED

*Words:* Annie Worsley
*Illustration:* Neil Gower

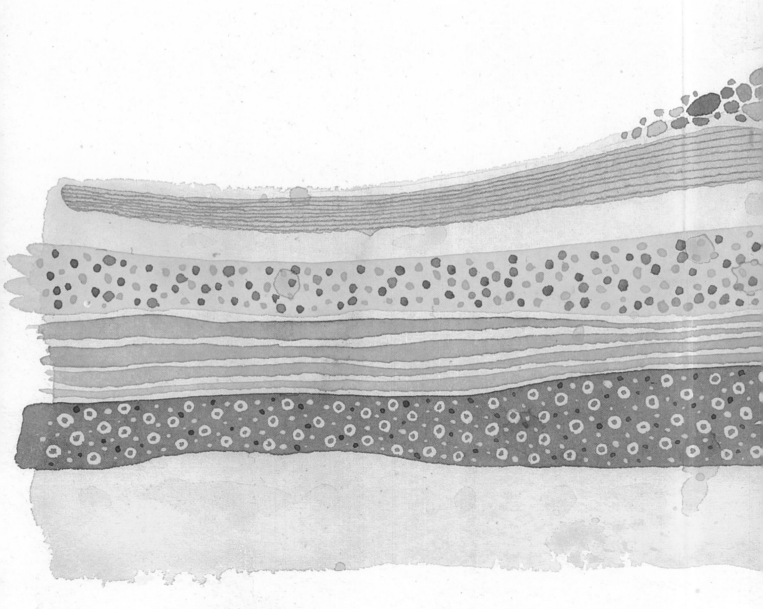

*From the Mull of Kintyre to the Highlands of New Guinea, the Stone Age craft of building a hearth and laying and setting a fire has remained unchanged over millennia.*

The geology and landforms of Scotland's western seaboard, from the Mull of Kintyre to Cape Wrath, are riddled and ridged with fjordic sea lochs, high cliffs, beaches and islands. In the south the long, thin Kintyre peninsula is bordered on its western side by the North Channel, which runs between the Atlantic and the Irish Sea, and on its eastern side by the Kilbrannan Sound. When my children were very small, we holidayed on its wilder, quieter eastern coast, finding solace and joy amongst remote beaches, strange rock formations and ancient sessile oak woodlands that were home to abundant wildlife.

One small, hidden beach close to Skipness Castle gazes down the full length of Kilbrannan Sound. In good weather it is possible to see the castle's twin across the sound at Lochranza on the Isle of Arran. Both buildings were constructed in the twelfth and thirteenth centuries using local foliated green-grey sedimentary rock, their windows, doors and corners decorated with pink Permian sandstone that must have been shipped across the water from Arran. A path runs through the castle grounds, past a roofless chapel filled with medieval gravestones and down to the shore. Here, lichens and sea thrift coat slabbed and sloping rocky outcrops, and shingle front-grazed meadows lead to pale grey-beige sands.

Secreted beyond the high walls enclosing the chapel and graveyard, and hidden from the rest of the world, is the sandy bay, no more than two hundred metres long.

Thirty years ago it was a place little visited, filled with songs of oystercatcher, plover and curlew, where my four children could play safely, happy knowing the beach was theirs. The first task, before sandcastle building or swimming, before any ball games or picnics, was to collect as much driftwood as possible and pile it up ready to make a fire. Brought on tides and waves driven by south-westerly winds, wood was plentiful then, plastic less so. Once a stock was gathered, the children helped to create a circular pit rimmed with big stones. They dug sand and collected an array of colourful rocks and cobbles, sized according to the strength of each small seeker, to place inside and around the hollow. More stones were piled on this side or that, depending on wind direction, until everyone was satisfied with the construction. With dried grass heaped below the smallest sticks, they each took a turn striking a match until the little pile was alight. Around the fire, all the gear a family needs for seaside picnics and play was haphazardly strewn about, and the spot became a temporary camp site.

Whilst the fire got going the children played, swam and ran, rushing back and forth to grab drinks or show off their best finds or complain that someone had not played fairly or another had splashed too vigorously. Birdsong melded with the excited melodies of kids, neither group distracted from their activities by the other. Once, we made a washing line with two sturdy sticks and a long piece of fishing twine the children had discovered tangled in the rocks. They hung their wet clothes to smoke as if curing salmon. Potatoes wrapped in tinfoil roasted under embers and hot stones, and when the fire died down the children toasted marshmallows on sticks.

This small beach scene was recreated for years wherever we holidayed. And we do it still. There are grandchildren now, and when they are old enough they too will learn the craft of building a hearth, laying and setting a fire, and toasting marshmallows.

During the hot summer of 2018, the whole family travelled en masse to the United States. The last of our children to be wed married a young woman from Ohio, and in the aftermath of the wedding celebrations we decamped together to the eastern shores of Lake Michigan to holiday in an old wooden clapboard and brick house. There, our simple marshmallow toasting was superseded by the creation of 's'mores'. Toasted in exactly the same way over an open fire, marshmallows are sandwiched between special biscuits known as 'grams' along with a piece of bitter chocolate. Heat from the singed mallow melts the chocolate, resulting in a warm, sticky, sweet treat. Our hosts insisted that the smoke from a wood fire built in a wild space, on a beach or in the woods, was essential. Descendants of pioneers of the American Midwest, they considered the making of s'mores to be one of the great outdoor initiations of kids in the backwoods of their home state. Whilst the gentle companionship of our newly extended family debated the finer details of what food is best cooked on an open fire, there was no argument about the way the fire itself should be constructed. Despite separation by thousands of miles, and differences in culture and history, we all used the same tried-and-tested method: a stone-henged and stone-lined fire.

A fire pit ringed by a henge of stones is an admixture of wood and rock, relics from once living trees and the remnants of ancient landforms – biosphere mixed with geosphere. There is a semi-permanent fire pit on the shore near my croft home in the Northwest Highlands. With my husband, I built a circular hearth of large rounded stones, wave-smoothed remnants of

Britain's most profound and remote geological past – gneiss, sandstone and quartzite streaked in dark green, purple, red, orange, pink, cream and glistening white. The coast faces west and occasionally we light a fire there and watch the sun slip away. And, at the cusp of day's transition to night, we have been joined by otters at their supper, seals drawn to fire-glow and birds settling down to roost around us.

Flames at the gloaming stir up memory and unsettle time – they draw in spirits of the past. Years before beach fires with my young family, I sat by another fire pit – sunken and lined with stones – baking sweet potatoes wrapped in large leaves. This hearth lay just inside the open entrance to a small hut made of wood, vines, leaves and grass thatch. Smoke spilled outside or rose up to seep through the roof and smouldering fires from other family huts nearby sent wraiths of pale vapour skyward. It was 1979 and as a young post-doctoral researcher I had travelled to the Highlands of New Guinea, nine thousand miles away from the UK.

At this time, most of the island's mountainous interior was still largely covered in jungle and unexplored. New Guinea lies north of Australia, straddling the equator, so its climate is tropical – heat and daily thunderstorms are exacerbated and exaggerated by high mountainous topography. Its position on the cusp of three tectonic plates means the island is geologically and geomorphologically active and unstable but rich in mineral and forest resources. In the 1970s most of the mountain ranges were covered by tropical rainforest dominated by trees such as the southern beech (*Nothofagus* species). These forests were, and in places still are, dense, luxuriant, richly diverse and pristine habitats, with enormous trees and deep soils. Communities were separated by volcanoes, deep gorges and dense forest, and travel between them was extremely difficult if not impossible. New Guinea contains a third of all global languages, reflecting both the

intense severity of the landscape and millennia of separation from the outside world. Although European traders visited coastal areas, the interior remained unexplored until the second half of the twentieth century – effectively, the Highlands of New Guinea were sealed off by their geography and geology.

In 1939 the Australian Leahy brothers flew across the Highlands and were surprised to see that amidst great swathes of montane jungle, mountains and deep gorges, several broad, relatively flat valleys appeared to have been partially cleared of woodland and contained organised agricultural communities. Eventually, in the 1950s, more organised exploration by Australian and European researchers began in earnest and soon small settlements with landing strips and Western-style buildings were established. Then came the search for mineral and forest riches, and with scientific and medical research came religion, education, Western-style commerce and lifestyles, and disease. Expeditions into the forests were greeted by tribal societies using what we think of in the West as Stone Age technologies – there were no metal implements and no pottery. Everything a community needed was hunted and foraged from the forests or grown in small, neat plots that Australian and European researchers termed 'gardens'.

I travelled to the island of New Guinea by means of a convoluted series of flights via the Persian Gulf, Sri Lanka and Hong Kong to the coastal capital of Papua New Guinea, Port Moresby, and then on to Mount Hagen village in the interior. It was my first ever journey by air. The final stage, in a small two-seater plane, plunging and plummeting between valleys and mountain peaks, was terrifying and nauseating. Mount Hagen was composed of several modern buildings and a section of dirt road called the Highlands Highway. There was a small tea and coffee research plantation and sturdy base camp huts for geologists, archaeologists, geographers,

ecologists and medics. For the first week I worked with my PhD supervisor and a team of archaeologists at the nearby Kuk Swamp. They had uncovered a complex array of ditches, mounds and settlement sites in swamp sediments below the contemporary wetlands. There were stone and wooden artefacts associated with horticulture, post holes denoting houses and hearths containing charcoal. Just as local villagers built houses and created fire pits in the 1970s, so prehistoric communities had done the same thousands of years before. Thus, in New Guinea, the technologies the West associates with the Stone Age extended back into deep time yet they were alive and well in the twentieth century.

At the Kuk site, remains of the remote past included evidence of early horticultural techniques in the form of man-made ditches close to natural palaeo-channels (channels made by rivers before the main phase of swamp development) and cultivated plots whilst layers of charcoal and artificial mounds were the very first signs of agriculture. Throughout the Holocene, communities practised elaborate and extensive water control – they domesticated yam, banana and taro and supplemented their diet by hunting and gathering. They built circular raised mounds for planting crops with complex networks of channels to drain water from the productive soil of the swamplands. Their tools were made from the raw materials of forest and mountain – there were stone axes and large wooden hafts, beautifully crafted wooden bows, small arrowheads and spears, and stones for cutting and grinding. Plant residues, such as starches and pollen grains, left on their surfaces and in sediments from across the site, yielded evidence of an ancient agricultural landscape that began at least ten thousand years ago and continued right through to the present.

Kuk is now a UNESCO World Heritage Site and renowned as an independent cradle of agricultural development and innovation, as unique and important as the Fertile Crescent of the Middle East. The peoples of the high remote mountains of New Guinea were amongst the world's earliest agriculturists. Their methods of cultivation, known as 'gardening' by visiting researchers, are truly ancient and their independent genesis is widely acknowledged by international scientific and archaeological communities. It is now recognised that the technologies developed in the Highlands have shaped cultures, populations and food supply throughout Oceania. For a while I stayed nearby with other scientists, proud to be helping with a project that even then was astonishing, its importance and significance mutually acknowledged between us all.

I then moved on, alone, to work on my own sites – small volcanic crater lakes close to Mount Giluwe (in the very centre of Papua New Guinea) from which precious mud had been extracted in long, thin cores. The lake mud contained pollen grains and spores from the plants of surrounding forests and gardens, volcanic ashes that could be used to date the various layers in a core, soil residues and other micro-fossils. From the oldest sediment at the bottom to the newest at the top, a timeline of vegetation and environmental history could be deduced from the differing natures of the mud and plant remains throughout the cores. And, by examining the pollen grain structure of key species such as the southern beech, it was possible to infer periods of soil in-wash from episodes of erosion of the lake catchment. A degraded pollen grain indicated that it had not been deposited directly onto surface water but onto soil and over time had been washed into the lake. Unlike lacustrine mud (found in lakes), soil is aerobic (containing oxygen), and oxidation is the only process that can damage or destroy the tough wall of a pollen grain. High amounts of degraded pollen suggested greater levels of soil erosion, whereas low numbers indicated stable vegetation. The evidence from my pollen studies was clear: the mounded gardens, drainage ditches and water management strategies had had little or no detrimental effects upon the forests of the New Guinea Highlands.

However, to understand how the populations and environments had developed over time, I needed to learn how Papuan communities used and interacted with the natural world, how they 'gardened', how they subsisted in such remote and difficult terrain, and why so little had changed over the millennia. My pollen data suggested that even in the most extreme landscapes of steep slopes and with intense rainfall, the forests had remained largely stable. Away from the newly emerging Western-style townships, people continued to use 'Stone Age' implements for clearing forests, building huts and hearths, gardening and food production, and warfare.

I stayed in a small hut built using the same methods that had been used for generations. A fire pit sat in the middle of the earthen floor just inside the entrance, designed in such a way that smoke seeped around the small internal space. On either side, away from the flames, were two small areas piled high with dried plants. One was my sleeping space, the other for a small semi-domesticated sow and her striped piglets. At night, when the drone of mosquitoes became almost unbearable, I took comfort in the thick sweet wood-smoke blanket and quilt of crisped leaves.

The hut stood in a tiny village perched on a small plateau above steep mountainsides, and there I was initiated into another way of life. I was taught how to build and keep my fire going, how to hunt, how to prepare food and cook using hot stones and embers, and how to 'garden'. Once an area of forest had been marked out for food production, trees were felled and used to make fences, house posts and tools. Undergrowth was slashed and heaped into great piles to be burned. All the piles eventually became mounds for growing crops, each one containing layers of ash and soil and rotting plant material – the perfect medium for growing food. Each mound was heaped in this way until it had a diameter of at least two metres. The layout of the mounds was akin to the honeycomb design of a bee's hive. Mounds were separated by ditches in which water would run downslope without eroding the precious soil. In the montane tropics afternoon deluges, developed in thunderstorms, rip soils away where vegetation is absent, but the elaborate design of mounded gardens meant that this was kept to a minimum. Rather than pass directly down steep slopes, creating gullies and washing away precious soil, the pattern of mounds meant that water moved laterally and diagonally, reducing its speed and potential for damage. The 'gardens' were productive and often maintained for several years before being allowed to go fallow. Some periods of fallow were for six months; others allowed the regeneration of secondary forest over twenty-five years or more, demonstrating the long-term planning by the villagers and the deep intergenerational understanding of how their environment functioned. This type of gardening had developed as populations grew, and early innovation allowed the people of Kuk to expand their cultivation onto the steep hillsides modifying the original ditch and mound systems of the swamplands.

Even before the true extent of Kuk's importance to agriculture in Oceania was evident, I knew instinctively that my small hut, with its permanently smouldering fire, was one small part of ritual and practical hearth-making stretching back in time over thousands of years. The scents and sounds of that place remain clear to me today, for my mind and body remember the 'Stone Age' of New Guinea. Once, as part of my initiation into village and tribal life, and also as a warrior, I was taken by two villagers deep into the forest almost a day's hike from where I was working. The walk was gruelling, hot, muddy and sweaty. I was covered in a mixture of grease and charcoal to fend off biting insects and leeches. We came to a small clearing and as we stood there people came out from the forest. Two of their warriors ran around me shouting aggressively, bows taught, arrows nocked. I was stiff with fear, for in 1979 the warfare that had long marked the Highlands was still common, but my companions said reassuringly that the people thought I was the ghost of an ancestor. Soon they were joined by women and children, who held out their hands in greeting, touching my body and calling out to others. I was led to a hut and we sat around a fire pit identical to the one in my own temporary hut-home.

My guides translated as best they could as I asked questions. What were their names? What food did they grow? Where did they hunt? The guides told them I was from a land far away. I was tall because I had been grown in a garden like theirs with my feet in a mound. I was pale because I carried all my ancestors with me. And I was like a baby, learning wisdom from the forest spirits. We shared food and exchanged smiles. I was given shells, a beautifully polished obsidian axe head and a spear. We offered the people a decorated gourd and a necklace made from tiny seeds. The fire smoked and my eyes watered fiercely. Forty years on and the scent of charcoal and sweet leaves and the glow of embers and food shared around a fire sweep me back to that traditional hearth in the forest.

Metal implements only arrived with Westerners during the second half of the twentieth century, but within a couple of decades the 'Stone Age' landscapes of the Highlands of New Guinea were being transformed at rates never seen before in the island's history. Forest clearance for roads, houses, schools, mines and plantations; logging and mining on enormous scales; the shift in culture from subsistence agriculture to monetary systems that disregarded the traditional methods of bartering. For many communities, development has brought considerable benefits though others lament the loss of a deep connection to the natural world.

In Britain, the Stone Age dwindled slowly over eleven millennia in the face of repeated waves of technological and agricultural developments from Europe. There are many archaeological sites across the British Isles where remnants of the 'lithic' past are preserved, some in wetlands remarkably like the Kuk Swamp. The stone-based technology in Palaeolithic Europe was no different from Stone Age technologies anywhere else in the world – hand axes found in deposits here are almost identical to those found in the tropical montane environments of New Guinea. In 2009 I worked on one small site on the Lancashire coast that yielded stone axe heads indistinguishable from my Papuan gift, along with smaller liths used as scrapers or arrowheads. They came from a camp site close to the prehistoric coast of Lancashire, some two miles from the present-day dune coastlands, on the edges of a palaeo-river channel (a buried palaeo-river, braided with channels). Micro-fossils extracted from the sediments enabled us to describe the environment in which those remote campers had settled – on a raised sand and gravel bank, next to an ancient river channel, surrounded by peat bogs and mixed woodland.

Amongst many post holes was a hearth – a pit of stones reddened by years of heat and bordered by a henge of guard stones. There was a cache of hazelnuts and a small 'carpet' made from woven rushes, and there were fragments of charcoal scattered around, remnants of the ancient fires. The hearth was of similar dimensions to the ones that kept me safe and warm in the remote high tropics and almost identical to the 'Stone Age' hearths of prehistoric New Guinea. And, with its little store of food treats and rush mat, I could easily imagine a fire side surrounded by happy children, just like the one in Kintyre where my family picnicked and played years ago.

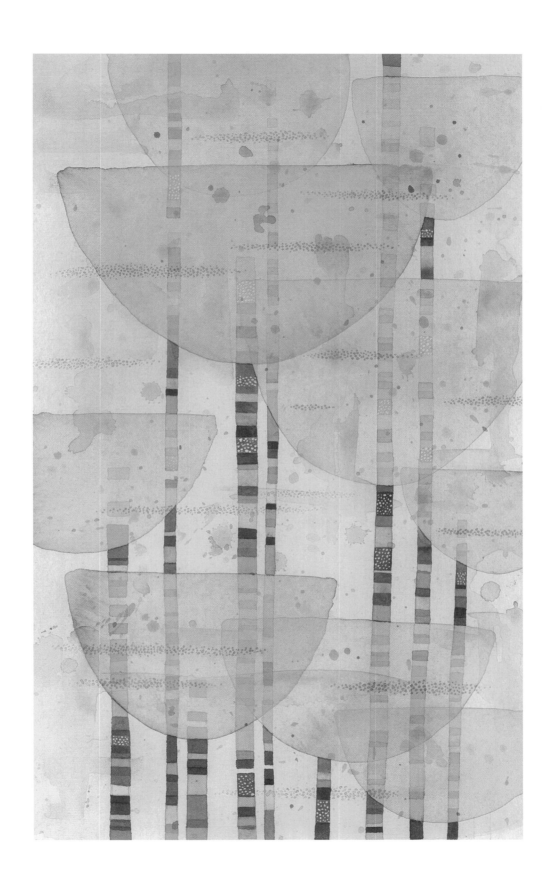

# TALISMANS AND TOMBSTONES

## ON COTTAGES, COUNTRYSIDE AND TINY CONSTRUCTIONS

*Words:* Sara Baume
*Photography:* Jay Armstrong

*Artist and writer Sara Baume makes miniature replicas of the grandiose mansions that brazenly adorned the Irish landscape of her childhood, conspicuous structures that stand in contrast to the traditional cottage sinking silently back into the soil.*

Of all the mass-produced souvenirs of Ireland – the cuddly sheep, the shamrock key chain, the Guinness candle, the plastic leprechaun, the harp-shaped fridge magnet – I harbour a particular affection for the Irish cottage figurine.

Typically, it's about as tall as a shot glass and no wider or longer than the palm of a hand. Painted the colours of thatch, whitewash and timber, it has a hipped roof, four low walls, two small, front-facing windows and a half-door. There might be flower boxes on the windowsills, a stack of turf against the wall, a bumpy garden of rocks and grass, a winding path trailing off the edge; there might even be a tiny lever protruding from a gable that, when gently cranked, plays a plinky-plonky version of 'Danny Boy'.

Whenever I refer to the miniature cottage, I carelessly, repeatedly use the word 'figurine', even though I know it's technically incorrect; a 'figurine' is most precisely an ornament depicting the human form. I use it involuntarily because it feels appropriate. There is something anthropomorphic about the cottage that other buildings lack – its heavy golden fringe and pale cheeks, its mouth hung slightly agog.

This summer I unearthed a photo-book called *Irish Cottages* from a cluttered stall in the weekly market of a coastal town close to where I live – a market that is in many ways symbolic of contemporary Ireland, swallowing the entire esplanade and peddling everything from fishing tackle, hardware and antiques to live ducklings, Indian spices and paper bowls of patatas bravas. The book is mostly composed of handsome photographs of cottages in unexpected variety; the introduction posits, compellingly, the idea of smallness as an architectural virtue. The first time I flicked through its pages, I experienced a strange gush of nostalgia. ⟫

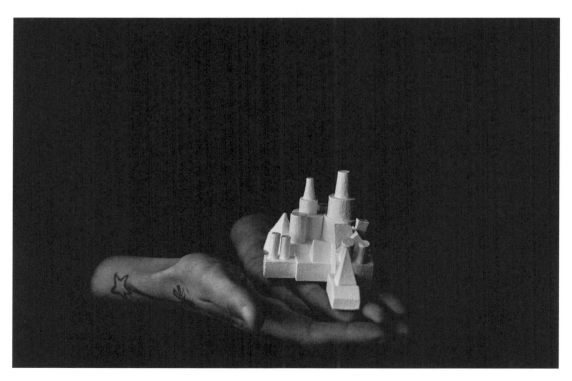

The pictures in the book were familiar to me and yet, at the same time, they were foreign.

*Irish Cottages* was published in 1990. Fourteen years later, in 2004 the British writer and environmental activist Mark Lynas published a long article in *The Guardian* entitled 'The Concrete Isle'. 'Forget what you've seen in the tourist brochures,' he starts, setting the tone. 'Today's reality is altogether different. If you want a tamed landscape dotted with off-the-shelf mock-Georgian houses, congested with nose-to-tail traffic and suffused by an ugly suburban sprawl, then *céad míle fáilte* – welcome to Ireland.' What follows is a compelling denunciation of the Celtic Tiger; Lynas describes a natural landscape as well as multiple sites of archaeological significance plundered by poor government and a generalised shallowness of morality. Though he interviews representatives of both sides of the argument, it's the voices of the Tiger's dissenters that make the most impact. 'What is going on across the board in this country is immensely destructive,' says Frank McDonald, then environmental editor of the *Irish Times*. 'The level of house-building spells catastrophe for scenic landscapes and the countryside in general if it continues.'

Smallness, evidently, is an aesthetic principle that was committed to Ireland's past during the years of economic prosperity or, at least, confined to the domain of the souvenir.

I didn't read Lynas' article in the year it appeared. In 2004 I was at university in Dublin, and I didn't return to live in the parish where I'd grown up for another four years. By then, it had conspicuously changed – an inordinate number of new houses had popped up, even a couple of little housing estates, and the volume of traffic passing through the crossroads outside my parents' house in the mornings and evenings had increased as a consequence, conjuring a soft and staggered sort of rush hour, flanked by cattle, barley and brambles.

At first, I was disgruntled about what I perceived to be a defilement of the landscape of the idyll of my childhood – the hacking down of trees I'd once climbed and the concreting over of grassy hills I'd once rolled down. These new houses stood in dramatic contrast to the vernacular architecture and even to the bungalows that had dominated from the 1970s to the early 1990s. Everything about them was incongruous. They were huge; sometimes more than a dozen windows pocked the facade, and they were spangled with unnecessary appendages – turrets, mock-fanlights, asymmetrical dormers and expansive conservatories. In addition, the homeowners, wherever possible, had chosen to situate their new country houses at the ends of protracted driveways and behind tall metal gates that opened electronically, majestically as their SUVs approached.

But, in the months leading up to the economic bust of 2008, my disgruntlement softened into curiosity. I developed a habit of sneaking around the parish where I had grown up taking photographs of the houses that were foreign to me. Later I made sketches of them, and later again I built miniature replicas out of miscellaneous scrap – rags, cardboard, timber offcuts, even straw. The idea was to draw a contrast between the grandiosity of the monster mansions and my choice of coarse, everyday materials – the intention being to invent an updated, and deeply cynical, souvenir.

'The Irish have never been an urban people by nature,' writes Marion McGarry in her book *The Irish Cottage: History, Culture and Design*. 'When we think of our major cities and towns they were variously founded by foreigners – Vikings or Anglo-Normans. To live in small groups in the rural countryside was part of Irish culture for generations.'

The cottage is the dwelling indigenous to our built environment – a structure that grew out of the soil like a bizarre knoll, a primordial rearrangement of rock and wood and straw. I can picture the apex of a chimney peeking up from the grass, followed by the ridge of the roof, the bristly trim, the stone walls and front-facing windows. It was composed of materials provided by the locality and designed in concord with the weather and environment, favouring level land and sheltered spots, facing away from the prevailing winds. And the Irish cottage licked substances out of nature to inflect itself with colour – limewash making white, copper sulphate making pale blue, slag deposits of iron making different shades of yellow and brown.

In the decade since the economic bust, I've continued to build miniature houses in some form or another, at times with purpose, though more often haphazardly. In the beginning each structure tended to be around the size of a dolls' house and reasonably representational; over time they have come to be smaller and more abstract. For my current series, entitled *Talismans*, each structure – like the Irish cottage souvenirs – is scarcely taller than a shot glass and roughly the length and width of the palm of my hand.

On the ground floor of the 'Country Life' exhibition at the National Museum of Ireland in County Mayo, there is a reconstruction of the interior of a nineteenth-century cottage. In summer 2018 I made a pilgrimage there to meet McGarry and to talk about indigenous architecture – or, perhaps, human behaviour.

'To understand Irish cottages is to understand this mindset of not standing out too much from the crowd,' McGarry writes, 'not showing off creature comforts, and not trying to elevate one's social status through the exhibition of a "taste" in architectural trends.' McGarry puts the cottage in context as a logical response to the modest needs of the people who lived off the land and sea – people who were poor, but only averagely so, and full of pride. The bungalow, for McGarry, represents a 'natural descendent' of the cottage in scale and shape, but she points

out how it soon came to be embellished by 'arches, concrete balustrades and stone cladding' and to be situated prominently, brazenly on the landscape, whereas cottages had more usually been hidden down lanes or surrounded by trees.

This mindset of utmost humility has completely transformed over the decades.

'Western identity,' McGarry continues in her book, 'has become increasingly associated with "the individual" as opposed to the "herd" attitude of our ancestors. With this came the ambition to reflect individuality and educated taste in one's home.' In *The Guardian* article of 2004 one of Lynas' interviewees is Ian Lumley, a heritage officer with An Taisce – The National Trust for Ireland. Lumley describes the Irish mentality as 'inherently anti-regulation and anti-officialdom'. He suggests that 'one of the theories is that this goes back to British occupation, to dodging the constabulary, dodging the revenue, getting away from the landlord, hiding pigs under the bed, hiding chickens in the roof and so on'.

These two contradictory factors combined – our historically fractious relationship with authority, in this instance levelled against regulations regarding the protection of environment and heritage, and our tendency to emulate the architecture of the old country houses of the ascendency – go some way towards explaining the proliferation of the monster mansions.

In the downstairs of the reconstructed cottage, McGarry showed me around the furniture and implements and explained the various meanings behind their arrangement.

In her book, she describes how 'the fire was both physically and socially situated in the centre of the house'. Whereas European families routinely gathered around the kitchen table, the Irish would push all of their furniture back against the walls to surround the light and heat of the hearth.

In the reconstruction, McGarry pointed out how most of the items owned by the cottage dwellers would have been sourced from natural materials – gorse was used as a brush to sweep the chimney, straw was woven to make chairs, dried cow pats were burned on the fire and the wing of a goose was used as a feather duster.

And then there was iron, which served multiple purposes – it was strong, practical and fireproof, but it was also believed to protect against 'faery' activity. Iron nails would be inserted into the walls of the cottage and horseshoes would be hung from a nail alongside the chimneys and windows and doors – any points at which the faery folk might be tempted to enter. A poker would be placed across a cradle to prevent the baby inside from being stolen.

Perhaps the feature that interests me most – and the piece of furniture whose form I am borrowing to build a display for my series of figurines – is the dresser, which was 'primarily a decorative piece' and 'a point of pride'. If you couldn't afford a dresser, McGarry told me, some kind of simpler alternative would always be fashioned, sometimes even just a shelf. For many decades in Ireland, strong pagan beliefs and rituals coexisted and even co-mingled with those of Roman Catholicism, and this is embodied by the 'holy shelf', which McGarry explains was 'traditionally reserved for the display of holy objects, statues and pictures, and lit with candles'.

I am very attached to this idea that no matter how meagre a person's way of life, it is essential to reserve a space for lining up those possessions considered to be most precious.

*Talismans*, as a completed installation, is a ten-metre-long horizon line of miniature houses, each carved from plaster to the rough scale of a cottage souvenir, but in the style of a contemporary rural dwelling – large, asymmetrical and endowed with an abundance of unnecessary appendages. At the beginning of the line-up the structures are recognisably house-like, but as the line proceeds they become increasingly abstract, and by the end each structure looks more similar to a stack of toy blocks than any kind of home. The horizon line is supported by a narrow shelf running along a wall of timber strips painted in temperate, domestic shades of yellow and trimmed, positioned and pinned to echo the tongue-and-groove panelling of a traditional dresser.

This installation is my most purposeful series of house-like structures to date; from summer 2017 to summer 2018, I sat for four or five hours most evenings cradling these small structures – first carving and later assembling them, and later again painting and repainting them. As I worked, I would listen to the radio and it was only towards the end of the project that I realised how the national news stories that had dominated that twelve-month cycle concerned the worsening housing crisis.

It was a year of rising rents, rising house prices, rising homelessness – and I had spent it shaping talismans as if by this means I might interpret my anxieties about the extinction of landscapes and the scarcity of sustainable homes; as if these miniatures and the process of their making might symbolise an attempt to protect against the future as well as to preserve the past.

As Ireland has changed, the mass-produced souvenirs intended to characterise and commodify it have changed in response, becoming more innovative and ironic. They now extend to include bog-flavoured air freshener, little jars of liquid luck, turf craft kits and instant Irish accent mouth spray.

Today there is, amongst Irish people, a renewed appreciation for our vernacular architecture and a return to the concept of building a house with sensitivity to its surroundings, though it feels to me like these acts of contrition have come too late. The majority of traditional cottages have already crumbled back into the undergrowth they sprouted from – their charming faces washed grey and blank by weather and time.

'Because of its strength,' McGarry writes, 'the chimney wall is one of the best preserved parts of many abandoned and ruined cottages'. And so the feature that once formed the hub of a family's movement and noise and warmth is now all that remains – planted silently into the soil, silhouetted smokeless against the sky, scattered across the Irish countryside like the headstones of untended graves or the standing stones of an ancient era – the earliest of all marks made on the land by human hands.

# HAVELOK'S TALE

## STORIES OF SETTLERS

*Words:* Eleanor Parker
*Illustration:* Lucy Eldridge

*The Old Norse place names that dot the map of northern and eastern England preserve the names of medieval migrants and Scandinavian voyagers. Though they left little trace of their presence, it is thanks to their descendants' storytelling that their personalities have become an enduring part of the land and language.*

There is a particular type of map that many people encounter early on in their study of Anglo-Saxon history. It can take various forms, but usually it looks like this: a map of England, divided in two by a wobbly line running diagonally west–east across the country, from the Welsh borders near Wroxeter to the Thames Estuary east of London. North of the line is a dense spattering of dots, making up no particular pattern, scattered all across the North but especially thickly clustered in Yorkshire, Lincolnshire and East Anglia. South of the line the map is empty, except for a few flecks that look like stray drops from a paintbrush.

This is a map of place names – specifically, names that illustrate the distribution of Viking settlement in England. The little dots are cities, towns and villages whose names show the influence of Old Norse, the language spoken by Scandinavian settlers who made their home in northern and eastern England in the ninth and tenth centuries. The wobbly line represents the southern border of what was later to be called the 'Danelaw', the area where Danish legal custom held sway. Today we call these people Vikings, but that word evokes a violent stereotype that is misleading here; most of the people who gave names to these English places were not Hollywood's idea of Viking raiders but farmers, landholders, neighbours and residents – settlers in a new home.

The language they spoke had a lasting effect on English and gave us a wide assortment of words that we still use today. They are mostly ordinary, everyday kinds of words, reflecting the integration of these settlers into the daily life of English-speakers. Some are very domestic – *egg, cake, knife, window* – and many are so basic it's hard to imagine the language without them: *husband, law, happy, gift*. Some are more poetic, though no less essential – just try writing about the English landscape without the Norse words *sky, fog, glitter* and *mire*. These and many more have their roots in Old Norse – including the word *root* itself – and every day we are speaking the language of those settlers, without even knowing it.

The places where they settled down, all over the north, also show the impact of their language. Either by making new settlements or by giving new names to places already there, they left their traces in each of those little dots on the map: the easiest to spot are all the names ending in *by* or *thorpe* or *kirk* across northern England. Those dots represent names, but they also show the presence of people – the clusters of people who have to live in a place and talk about it, to each other and to their neighbours, before the name they have given it is sufficiently well known to last.

One of those dots represents the place where my grandmother was born – Wrangle, a tiny village in southern Lincolnshire. I always thought its name was a bit odd – in a nice way – and after learning about that map I understood why it looks so different from the names I grew up with in southern England. It comes from Old Norse and means something like 'crooked' or 'twisted'; it might once have referred to the shape of a piece of land or a nearby river. It is related to *wrong*, another word we got from Old Norse, and another word it's hard to imagine doing without.

Many of these settlements are named after people and preserve the name of a Norse landowner in some form or other. Not far away from Wrangle is Skegness, which probably takes its name from a Scandinavian man named Skeggi; then there's Ormskirk from Ormr, Scarborough from Scarthi, and many more. This type of name is my favourite, and it was what amazed me when I first encountered that map, a decade ago or more. In most cases we know nothing about these people except their names, but those names have become part of the landscape and may endure as long as the land itself lasts. These places bear the names of people who died over a thousand years ago, who left no other trace of their presence on earth.

In the later Middle Ages, some of these communities were aware that the names of their towns had an origin of this kind. They probably didn't know any more about their namesakes' lives than we do, but they found the names a spur to the imagination – a prompt to a story, an opportunity to weave a tale about where their town came from. Long after the Vikings had receded into history, it was possible to reconstruct the settlers' story out of the names they had left behind.

In one part of Lincolnshire, this developed into a legend that became profoundly important for the area's sense of its history and identity. This was the story of Grim, a Danish fisherman who was said to be the founder, father and namesake of the town of Grimsby. Grim's story seems to have been widely known in medieval Lincolnshire, and was often taken to be factual history (though if there is any historical basis for the story, no one has ever been able to discover it). It is most vividly recorded in a Middle English poem called *Havelok*, which was probably written in Lincolnshire in the thirteenth century. This is a poem I've come back to many times, and keep coming back to, though in some ways it's a very simple tale. It's almost a fairy tale, and like the best fairy tales it has a quality about it that touches deep currents in the human heart. Above all, it celebrates the ties of family and home, and a connection to place. In this poem, the relationship between the Danish characters and the land they settle in becomes almost a sacred union, a powerful bond of reciprocal love.

Let me tell you the story. It begins with two orphaned children: a little girl named Goldburh and a little boy named Havelok. Goldburh is the daughter of the king of England and Havelok the son of the king of Denmark, but royal birth can't save them from tragedy, and they lose their parents whilst they are still children. Both are given into the care of guardians, and both are betrayed: Goldburh's wicked guardian imprisons her and takes control of her kingdom, whilst Havelok's protector decides to kill him. He gives the young prince to a fisherman, Grim, and orders him to be drowned. But Grim – like Snow White's huntsman – can't bring himself to kill the child, so he and his wife give up their livelihood and their home to take Havelok to safety in England.

They flee by boat from Denmark and are driven by a favourable wind to land on the banks of the Humber. There Grim constructs a small, rough-and-ready dwelling and works hard at his trade to make a new life for his family. The poem glories in Grim's work, lovingly detailing the fish he catches in the fruitful waters of the North Sea: sturgeon, herring,

mackerel, turbot and so on. Not many poems would take the trouble to list the names of the fish, but this is a poem that finds meaning in the everyday, in loving attention to the details of daily life. In Grimsby, always a fishing town, it must have seemed only right that the town's founding father should have been a prosperous fisherman.

Through Grim's labour, both his family and their new home thrive, and so, the poem tells us, the settlement beside the Humber takes its name from him: it becomes known as Grimsby, the name it will have 'until Doomsday'. The young prince Havelok grows up having to work for his living, with no expectation of regaining his kingdom. He is a lovable boy, cheerful and good-tempered, not especially clever but very tall and strong. As he grows up, he eats too much for Grim to easily keep him, so he makes his way southwest from Grimsby to Lincoln, where he gets a job as a kitchen boy. From there the story unfolds in true fairy-tale style. The wicked earl who has imprisoned Goldburh sees a way to humiliate the princess by marrying her, against her will, to this sturdy peasant lad, and so Havelok and Goldburh are married, very reluctantly. But – to cut a long story short – of course they fall in love, win back their kingdoms and live happily ever after.

*Havelok* is a poem that is full of love: love for family, for home, for work and for the bonds that these different strands of human experience form for us. Havelok begins the story as a helpless orphan, but wherever he goes he has the ability to forge enduring ties of friendship. Almost as soon as he loses his birth family, he finds a loving foster family in Grim and his wife and children, who take him in and support him right to the end of the story. Havelok and Goldburh become a devoted and mutually supportive couple, and at the end of the poem we're told they have fifteen sons and daughters – a happy ending for two orphans who have lost all other family. All the people Havelok meets in his poverty, who help him when he has nothing to give them in return, become his closest supporters and dearest friends, even after he regains his kingdom.

This is the story of an exiled prince and princess, but at heart it is about ordinary working people: fishermen, merchants, cooks and kitchen boys. These are the kinds of people who are hardly ever given an important place in medieval literature, or in most literature, but *Havelok* cares deeply about them and about their world. Most medieval narratives that share the same basic plot as *Havelok* – a dispossessed nobleman fighting to win back his inheritance – treat the place where the hero spends his exile as a temporary and not very important part of the story. If an Arthurian knight wanders abroad into strange lands on a quest, he always comes home to his own court; if he has to spend time working in a menial job, what matters is how he gets out of the situation, not what happens to him whilst he's there. Arthurian knights don't care where the food on their table comes from, and the people whose labour produces it are usually invisible – often it appears literally by magic. *Havelok* is not like that. England begins as Havelok's place of exile, but it becomes his home. Unlike some medieval heroes, Havelok does not just play at being a poor kitchen boy working for his living in Lincoln: that's what he really is, and the poem is proud of it.

The poem is proud of its roots, too: proud of being from Lincolnshire, of being the story of Lincoln and Grimsby. It talks fondly of Lincoln and celebrates the town that bears the name of Grim, the hardworking fisherman who raises his family, fosters his little settlement into a thriving town and saves the life of a future king. Naturally enough, the story of

Grimsby's foundation recorded in this poem was long remembered in Grimsby itself. It was given pride of place on the town's medieval seal, which shows Grim, Havelok and Goldburh: Grim, the tallest of the three figures, is holding a sword and shield, with the little king and queen sheltering under his protective arms. As late as the nineteenth century, stories were still being recorded from Grimsby about Grim – 'Old Grime', as they called him – which even then imagined him as the town's protector, saving it from an attack out at sea. Grim was remembered as his town's father and defender, just as he becomes Havelok's beloved foster-father in the poem.

Beyond regional pride, there are other ways in which love of place seems to be particularly important in this legend – a deeper connection, which verges on the sacred and reaches back to ancient ways of thinking about the bond between places and the people who inhabit them. When Grim gives his name to the town of Grimsby in the poem, it symbolises something more profound than a simple act of settlement. This is a story with its roots in Viking legend, and there, as well as being an Old Norse personal name, Grim is a pseudonym of the god Odin. In Norse myth, Odin is a wandering god who walks the earth in disguise, half hooded, and takes many names in his interactions with humans. In Norse sagas, young heroes facing crucial moments of danger may suddenly meet a mysterious old man who gives them aid or magical gifts, and this stranger usually seems to be Odin, though it is not always stated plainly. Perhaps somewhere behind the kindly fisherman Grim of *Havelok* is a memory of some older legend, where the Grim who saves Havelok's life by spiriting him across the North Sea is actually Odin in disguise.

If Grim is founder and father of Grimsby, Havelok's connection to home is something different: he is the rightful king of Denmark, and at some point in his story, even if he is content to be a happy kitchen boy, the logic of such tales as this says he will have to return to the kingdom he has left behind. At a crucial moment in the poem, Havelok has a dream that awakens him to this potent, yearning love for home.

He dreams he is seated on a hill, looking out over his country and all its people, and he imagines himself stretching out his arms to embrace them, drawing them towards him like a lover. Then the dream shifts and he is holding them within his closed hand, flying with them across the sea to England. There he opens his hand and presents them, as a gift, to his new wife.

The word Havelok uses to describe this embrace is one I like very much: 'I fathomed Denmark,' he says, 'with my long arms'. Here the poem is using the older sense of the word 'fathom', meaning 'to encircle with the arms'. The word came to be a measurement of distance, because a 'fathom' was the length of a person's outstretched arms (generally taken to be equal to six feet); today we associate this word with measurements of depth, perhaps with plumbing the depths of the sea, and therefore, in a metaphorical sense, with understanding and the process of coming to know something. But in *Havelok* it refers to a more intimate gesture than that, involving the space within the arms, against the breast, near to the heart. To 'fathom' someone was to embrace them and hold them close, like a parent with a child, a lover with their beloved.

That kind of tender embrace is what Havelok imagines as he dreams of his home, the land itself and all the people who inhabit it. When he tells Goldburh of his dream, she understands it to be a prophetic sign calling him home: they must go back, liberate his people from the unjust usurper and restore the rightful king. Perhaps here too there is a shadow of an older kind of myth: the king who gives his body to the land, a sacred kingship born of the union between blood and earth. To rule a place is not just to have power over it but to love it, sacrifice for it, become one with it.

When I think about Havelok's dream, I imagine standing on a particular hill near where I live in rural Oxfordshire. Rising above the Thames, this hill gives me a view over the whole surrounding countryside, with the river glittering as it makes its way between the fields and villages. From there I can see the place where my grandmother lived after she left her Lincolnshire home, when she moved away from Wrangle and came south to marry. Her life in that new home, for all its pastoral beauty, proved to be a difficult one: within a few years she was a single mother, bringing up four children alone. They were poor, and she worked hard to support them with the twentieth-century equivalent of the exhausting jobs Havelok laboured at in medieval Lincoln – cleaning houses, stacking shelves in Tesco. It's that kind of work, day after day, that forms and sustains families and homes; it may not be as dramatic an act of home-building as the foundation of a new town, but it nonetheless deserves to be celebrated and remembered.

For me that family connection is bedded deep into this Oxfordshire landscape, the area that is now my home. From high up on that hill, my home looks so small that it does indeed become possible to imagine taking it in my hand and holding it in my arms, as Havelok does with Denmark. Except in dreams, we can never do anything of the kind – and yet the image expresses how strongly we crave a physical connection to the places we love, wanting to make a tangible thing of that most intangible of concepts, home. Unlike Grim and those Scandinavian settlers in the Danelaw, not many of us will give our names to our homes so that they bear the signs of our presence 'until Doomsday'. But we all have places that we love, and one of the most powerful ways to bond ourselves with them is to tell stories about them, imagining what made them what they are, and what makes us part of them.

I come back to Havelok's word 'fathom' – the wide-armed embrace, which is also, for us today, a word that suggests a deepening process of understanding. When you open your heart to a place, as Havelok opens his arms, you do come to fathom it in both of those senses: nothing fosters knowledge of a place like allowing yourself to become at home there. Perhaps telling a story about your home, as the people of medieval Grimsby did, is a way of fathoming it in every sense, coming to understand it and drawing it closer to your heart.

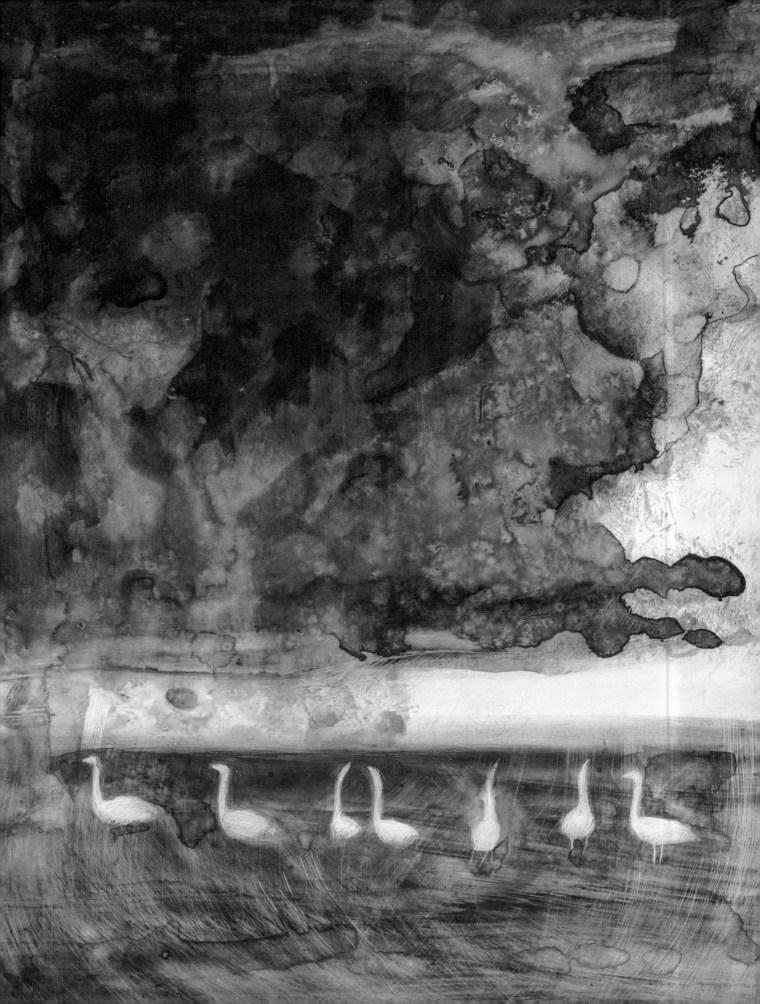

# LISTENING
# TO THE LAND

---

## ON THE WINGS OF WILD SWANS

*Words:* Jim Crumley
*Illustration:* Catherine Hyde

*Where Highland and Lowland Scotland meet, a flock of wintering whooper
swans listen to the land and speak with a single voice. Leaning into the
earth and listening intently take us far beyond the simple act of hearing.*

The first time I ever became aware of the possibilities of listening to the land, I was watching a flock of whooper swans. What happened was this…

I was driving through my back-of-the-hand landscape of the upper regions of the River Forth, with the southernmost mountains of the Highlands immediately to my north – that Lowland-into-Highland terrain where I have scratched a nature writer's living for more than thirty years now, the Highland Edge. It has always been a fruitful landscape for a nature writer because here, where Highland and Lowland Scotland collide, the wildlife tribes of both realms overlap, and sometimes the distinctions between their preferred habitats blur, making almost anything possible. The land around the upper reaches of the Forth is flat, though it soon rises abruptly in every direction but east.

As I drove slowly south between hedges full of hunting parties of tree sparrows and the glowing egg-yolk light of yellowhammers perched like candles all along the hedge, I saw a flock of whooper swans in the next field. I should explain that I have a thing about swans, that I have devoted a disproportionate amount of time and ink in pursuit of the secrets of their often surprising lifestyle. If pushed I would concede a particular affinity with whoopers, with their northern wildness, with the grace of all Arctic travellers wherever they touch down.

The hedges are tall, but if you have a small four-wheel-drive car with good ground clearance and if the roads have generous ditch-free grass verges (I have and they do), then you are well placed to sneak gently and confidently into a position from which you can watch a field of swans without getting out of your mobile hide. I

duly sneaked into position, lowered the nearside window, switched off the engine. At once the gentle muted brass conversation of whooper swans drifted in on the breeze. I should further explain that this was a practised manoeuvre, that I have watched swans hereabouts for years and that I knew that this flock had been growing slowly from an original handful, and by erratic increments over about two weeks, until now there were the better part of two hundred. Wherever they roosted at night (possibly on the river, more likely the shallow loch a few miles to the west), they returned each day to the same field. When wild creatures settle into a routine like this, they grow confident, and they can accommodate a careful, unthreatening human presence at relatively close quarters, especially with the barrier of the hedge between us. The nearest birds were about twenty yards away, the furthest about a hundred yards. They were relaxed and feeding on some of the best grass in the land.

Towards midday, a deep calm settled on the flock, a mood almost as visible as a cloud. A few birds grazed on but most dozed or preened half-heartedly. Some simply sat, in a posture that reduced the shape of a head-on swan to a low, wide dome from the crown of which protruded an erect neck topped by a wedge-shaped head. I tried to sketch it but my incompetence as an artist meant I was quite defeated by its symmetrical simplicity. But the great virtue of sketching is that you look harder, and you see better. And I realised then that there is one essential difference between whooper swans and mute swans when they gather in flocks. The mutes remain a loose assembly of individuals, but whoopers behave as a coherent and disciplined flock, for the rituals of migration have bred in them the capability of reaching collective decisions and acting on them collectively. I now saw this phenomenon stir, a sudden breath of awareness. The apparently imperturbable nature of that mood of calm was revealed in an instant as a thin veneer cloaking a perpetual state of tense awareness. The flock raised its many dozing heads, sitting birds suddenly stood.

The problem appeared to be in the west, for every head strained that way. I turned my binoculars on land and sky and found nothing. I had thought perhaps a hen harrier was scouring the edge of the field. The harrier is a bird that always unsettles swans, although it's hard to imagine how it could be conceived as a threat. Perhaps the slowness of its flight simply unnerves. There was no hen harrier. But the swans were undoubtedly troubled by something. Their questioning 'woo-pah?' calls spread through the flock, with an interrogatory edge to the second syllable. Then, slowly, they began to relax – they sat, heads and necks still tall, still facing west, still attentive. It was then that I realised that every bird was listening. I recognise that moment now as crucial to the evolution of my nature-writing life, one that would come to redefine my relationship with nature, with the very land itself.

Then the birds began to stand again, their voices raised, their anxiety palpable. I could still see nothing, and when I consciously tried to listen, I could still hear nothing. Once again, the birds sat, and for several minutes more they simply stared west, listening. Then they were on their feet again, and this time there was no mistaking the problem, for now their alarm coincided with a peal of thunder. The swans had been responding to the approach of a storm when it was still under the horizon, listening to it when it was still beyond the reach of human ears. The storm advanced as a grey-black wall. Thunder, lightning and thudding rain all tormented the swans, but they neither flew nor sought cover. Instead, they sat and pointed their beaks up into the rain. They cried out at every thunderclap, but ignored the lightning. When it was over, they stared east after the storm, and clearly the thunder still carried to their ears long after it had passed beyond the reach of mine.

In the weeks, months, years and decades since that day, its lesson has grown on me, grown in significance, grown into a kind of first commandment. So now my listening goes far, far beyond the simple act of hearing. Because consciously listening to the land has the curious consequence of uniting all your senses and bringing them all to bear on your surroundings with an acute focus.

When I was a young newspaper journalist (very young – I started at age sixteen), I soon began to nurture dreams that one day I would slip the yoke of newspapers and write my own literature of the land, dreams that were fostered by chance encounters with the works of three writers of genius – Gavin Maxwell, Marion Campbell and George Mackay Brown. Maxwell's *Ring of Bright Water* electrified me when I first read it, aged about eighteen. Almost its first words articulated the truth that we suffer as a species because of the distance we have put between ourselves and nature. I immediately read it again, and thought: 'I want to do that.' That was the seed, my first lesson in the art of writing landscape.

Marion Campbell's book *Argyll: The Enduring Heartland*, written over forty years ago, is still one of the finest books about Scotland that I have ever read. She would become a great friend and, when she died aged eighty in 2000, I read a poem from that book at her funeral.

She was an archaeologist as well as a sublime writer. A favourite passage begins:

> *To understand a landscape one must learn its bones. Rock gorge and flood plain,*
> *ice-smoothed hill or upthrust ridge record the earth's experience like wrinkles on*
> *an old face… The underground bones control the growth above, the green skin of*
> *earth revealing what lies below.*

Argyll was in her bones and her heart – her family were in the same part of the county for four hundred years – but her gift was to make the particular speak for all landscapes. I fancy she did not just listen to her landscape – she conversed with it, exchanging immortal truths.

George Mackay Brown, without being a nature writer in the accepted sense of the term, also exudes a sense of place – Orkney – in his every utterance. In a vocabulary all his own, he weaves nature symbols and man-made symbols together, almost like breathing: lark, hawk, star, cornstalk, swan, eagle, wind, sun, loom, seal, harp, plough, daffodil, ox…

Like all the great stylists, his voice is instantly recognisable:

> *In the first darkness, a star bled.*

No author ever leaned closer to the land. He remains unquestionably my favourite writer.

These three, then, prepared the ground long before the swans in the field taught me to listen. The location of the swan field was crucial, for it lies at the southern edge of what I have since come to think of as my nature writer's territory, my wild hearth. It extends north from there over the foothills and into those southernmost Highland mountains: Balquhidder Glen is its heartland and Glen Dochart its northern edge. At various times in these last thirty years, I have lived on its southern edge, its northern edge or in its heartland, working and reworking the same set of landscape circumstances again and again and again, for the priceless thing you acquire when you work that way is intimacy. Over time – and everything of value in our relationship with nature needs time – you acquire a sense of natural rhythms, of how nature moves across a particular landscape. As a result, when something new happens, you notice, so when you travel far beyond your idea of a home territory, you find that the principles are transferable, that the particular in nature becomes the general. I have found in other northern landscapes – Alaska, Iceland, Norway, Shetland – that the thought processes derived from listening to land I know well in the heart of Scotland stand up to scrutiny. All across the northern hemisphere, nature speaks with a single voice.

I have never believed that the land is neutral. I think it reaches out to us, offers guidance – I think it is accessible to us, if only we are willing to relearn the lost art of listening to it. Perhaps the most revealing evocation of that idea comes from Barry Lopez in his remarkable book *Arctic Dreams*. He argues for the appreciation of the land as having its own identity, that we should 'approach it with an uncalculating mind, with an attitude of regard' and that we should take the time and trouble to discern the variety of its moods and the creatures it sustains. He also spells out how the land rewards us for our efforts to understand it: one singularly revealing moment 'and you know the land knows you are there'.

There it is. You know the land knows you are there.

That is the goal. The land treats you as one of its animals. And then, your next task – what Lopez calls 'the pursuit of something sacred revealing itself' – is to have the animals treat you like part of the landscape.

I have been deeply immersed in writing a tetralogy of the seasons, a five-year-long project of four volumes that began with *The Nature of Autumn*, out of which would flow in their own good time *The Nature of Winter*, *The Nature of Spring* and *The Nature of Summer*. It is by far the most ambitious project I have tackled. Its landscapes range widely across Scotland from Galloway and the Pentland Hills in the south to Shetland in the north. From hardcore Highlands such as the Black Mount and Rannoch, to the islands of Colonsay and Harris and Iona in the west, and Glen Clova in the east. It dips exploratory toes into English waters at Lindisfarne and into the Lofoten Islands of Arctic Norway. But much of it is rooted in that Highland Edge territory where I learned to listen to the land.

One of the themes common to all four books is the erratic nature of what the seasons have become – the trauma our species is inflicting on nature, on the land itself. I wrote in The *Nature of Autumn* about a disturbing day in the immediate aftermath of Storm Abigail in November 2015. I had gone out to inspect the havoc she had wreaked on the nearer parts of my territory. As I drove home in near darkness through squalls that rocked the car, it occurred to me that what I had seen of Abigail's wrecking spree was surely a tiny symptom of something much, much larger – something oceanic, something global. I wrote in a notebook, 'nature is restless'. The next day I walked familiar woods, a favourite lochside and the lower slopes of the mountain I know best. I have watched forty years' worth of seasons unfold here, and never seen the place in such a seething, tortured mood. All I can say with any certainty about what I picked up on that day was that it felt like something much larger than the confines of what I could see. My response to that thought was to sit and listen. I found a place beside a waterfall on a mountain burn with a wide view over the upper glen. Young Scots pines were hand-planted there a few years ago, and they have now begun to fulfil the promise of a recreated pinewood. Above the glen, a shattered boulder field soars steeply to within a few hundred feet of the mountain summit. There I sat, and there I listened.

My ambition for that hour was to become a part of the mountain. If anything, that sense of nature in a mood of distressed restlessness was more marked than the day before, or at least I felt it more keenly. It felt as if nature itself was nearing a fundamental watershed, beyond which the land would be changed utterly and forever. That evening, I heard for the first time about the potentially catastrophic change in the behaviour of Zachariae Isstrom, a colossal glacier in northernmost Greenland, and shuddered with a kind of recognition. Climate scientists at the University of California had just announced that it is melting, at the rate of five billion tons a year. It is being compromised from above and below by increasing air temperatures and warming ocean currents. The scientists also suggested that it will retreat northwards by twenty to thirty kilometres – into the coldest part of northernmost Greenland – over the next twenty to thirty years.

But how might that colossal but distant turmoil communicate itself to a solitary nature writer sitting at the foot of a mountain in the heart of Scotland? How might it communicate itself to you, for that matter? Dare I suggest, perhaps on the wings of wild swans? No creature that comes into our midst knows more about the Earth's northernmost islands and oceans, no creature listens more attentively to the speech of that land, and no creature is more sensitive to what is at risk in our hemisphere than those wintering whooper swans on the edge of a Stirlingshire field, or at Caerlaverock on the Solway Firth, or further south in the Fens or at Slimbridge. We may not be able to interrogate them about the truths they undoubtedly understand, but at the very least we can see them as nature's ambassadors from the northlands of the world, as the most potent of symbolic reminders that what befalls those northlands will not stay there, because it never does.

All of which makes me wonder about that restlessness I felt sitting by the waterfall under the mountain. It was as if Abigail had shaken up an old order and laid out the beginnings of something ominous and new. Nor did it stop there. She proved to be the first of a series of storms that charged through the winter, flaying the land and piling floodwater on floodwater. And it began in a quiet mountain glen in the heart of my country the same day that a Greenland glacier made headlines all round the world.

The bottom line is that we have to listen.

You have to listen.

I have to listen.

The whole world has to listen, for the land's message is easy to understand in any language. Any wild whooper swan can tell you that.

# ARGYLL – THE ENDURING HEARTLAND

## LANDSCAPE WITH FIGURE

*Words:* Marion Campbell
*Illustration:* Catherine Hyde

*'The bond holds fast between home-ground and people,' wrote archaeologist and author Marion Campbell (1919–2000), who spent almost her entire life on the headland of Kilberry in Argyll, western Scotland, devoting herself to its prehistory and environment.*

It is very early on a summer's day. Last night a saffron band lay along the northern ridge at midnight, heat-heavy leaves drooping black against it under a faint star. Westward and seaward the tide fetched in the haze until a white mist hid the water. Now the mist has rolled, heavy as the pulled locks of fleeces, over the white sand where the terns drowse; it has coiled above the machair and eased the small herbs' thirst; it has filled every gully and billowed up the steep face of the grass cliff. Below the fenced edge of the field it spreads in a level carpet. It hides the sea, letting only a fret and a whisper rise through the blanket from which erupt the sleepy heads of islands.

At the inland side of the field a gate opens. A man leaves the trees for the open ground.

The mist has hidden the hayfields and veiled the deep green of growing corn. The cattle are up on the rough parks, the sheep lie cudding their dawn feed. The only animal afoot is this one, treading the dew-wet grass.

As he walks steadily to the headland a gull drifts above him, a redshank pipes from the hidden shore, a pair of curlews float from the hill with that tui-tui… tui-tui-tui that wrenches the exiled heart. Man and birds are thirled to the turning tide, and they go now to seek their livelihood.

The tide itself once washed where now the mist lies, at the lip of a shelf carved by cold seas out of glacial drift, in that long age when land and sea played a slow see-saw and the rocks escaped from their vast ice-coffins. That was before the hunters came north and westwards from the lands where their far ancestors had caught Rhône salmon or chased the wild bulls of Altamira.

When the first man trod this ground is still an unanswered question; perhaps he came towing a sledge and hooded in deerskin to fish among the floes where the fat shoals swam; perhaps he traversed bleak tundra from pocket to stunted pocket of scrub-willow; perhaps already he braved the open sea.

Whenever he came, it was a while back even as rocks and sea count time – ten thousand years or so, give or take a summer. The sea had carved caves in the rocks above the newly lowered shoreline and left them neatly paved with storm-laid cobbles. There he could camp, or he could rig on the short turf of the sandy machair his rounded tent of skins.

They knew no abiding city, these firstcomers, nor could they have borne a fixed abode. It was in their hard-won skills to move with their food-supply, following deer to the narrow pass and seals to the breeding-reef, gulls to the loch and fish to the shallows. At a rich hunting-ground they might team with another band to cull whatever plenty was there; in lean times they must scatter far afield and make the best of anything they could find.

The seasons returned them to favoured camps, to add to last year's heap of shells and clean-picked bones, or to a sheltered cave with its spalls of worked flint on the sunny side of the entrance. They were themselves the rarest animals in their environment - many a brown bear and many a stag lived out its days without once snuffing the taint of woodsmoke.

Neat-footed, deft-handed, makers of the smallest of stone tools to arm their antler harpoons, they have not left us even the bones of their dead to show their stature (let alone their skin colour); as for the rich store of custom and ritual that most hunting-peoples use, that is gone beyond recall. We who like to fancy ourselves masters of the world should stop to wonder how we would fare in a trackless country, where the only food that did not see and hear better, and run faster, than we could, would be clammy shellfish and such plants or nuts as we could risk eating.

It's a skilful business, the really simple life, and most of us have lost the skills, though some basic thoughts remain. The control of man by his environment – not the other way about – is something the Gael remembers. His words for land and people are interchangeable, and he will tell you he 'belongs' to Skye or Islay or Knapdale; he, or his grandparents, may have left the home-ground, he may have been born in Glasgow or Toronto, but the bond holds fast.

Watch the sheep. They live on the heather, four or five acres of moorland to every ewe. We round them up and drive them to the fank for dipping and clipping and dosing for their manifold ills – many a harassed farmer thinks they spend their leisure dreaming up new diseases – but you will not see us driving them back to the hill. A gate is opened, a dog called to heel, and out trots the first old ewe. A white woolly ribbon of her sisterhood forms up behind her and unwinds towards the braeface; six turn along the ridge, five ford the burn, eight head for the pass… long before twilight each of them will be back in her own chosen place. She will drop her lamb, most likely, at the rock where she was lambed; if you offer her an easy old age in a lush pasture, she will butt and scramble her way home to ensure its birthright for her last lamb. She is 'hefted to that hirsel', as we say, and the Gael is hefted too.

We are not the masters. The land dictates its use to all but the stubbornest of men, and most of all in hill-country where the sea has bitten deep. Here, and here only, can one cross the ridges; here is the ford; there a boat will lie safely on good holding-ground.

When the ice-fed sea was highest it made a bay of Crinan Moss and an inlet of Glassary Glen; Knapdale was an island, Kintyre another. The eighteenth-century droveroads followed ancient trackways marked by standing-stones, and the feet of travelling men turned aside to cool springs long before, and long after, the wells were guarded by rock-cut crosses. Man uses what he can find, but the skill is in the finding.

And now that solitary figure has crossed the field and vanished into the thinning mist. An engine putters into life; presently the boat appears, far out in a clear patch of sea, a narrow shape piled high with lobster-creels. Or are they creels, and is there an engine? Is it not some lean dark hull that brings old fears to land, or the curach of an Irish saint, or even a sealskin-and-whalebone kayak bearing the first bold seafarer?

The curlews might know, but they are busy on the tidewrack. Two gulls attend the boat – they know. The rabbits have come out on the machair as it warms under the sunrise, but it is no good asking them – they are Johnny-come-latelies with less than two hundred years to their credit or discredit.

And as for me, I can only tell it as I saw it, on a summer's morning, very early.  ✺

# LEARNING TO LOOK OUTSIDE

MY HOME, MY SKETCHBOOK AND ME

*Words & Illustration:* Nicola Davies

*Stifled for many years by perfectionism, a writer's deep desire to express her love of nature through art is rekindled by a new landscape. With it comes an understanding that what matters most is the simple act of picture making and the relationship between place and artist.*

When I was nineteen, like many students of my generation, I read John Berger's *Ways of Seeing*. It felt like looking into a pool of clear water and seeing the world stilled, magnified, in a kind of hyper-focus. After forty years, that sense of looking at the world through a new kind of lens has remained, but almost all the details have faded, except one: this wonderful thought about the nature of seeing, with love:

*When in love, the sight of the beloved has a completeness which no words and no embrace can match: a completeness which only the act of making love can temporarily accommodate.*

It has stayed with me partly because, like most nineteen-year-olds, I was in love when I first read it, but also for another, odder reason: it somehow expressed how I had felt for years about landscape, particularly the landscape around my parents' house in Suffolk, where I'd spent my adolescence. The fields, green lanes and hedgerows within a two-mile radius of that house were my beloved. I had spent hours, years gazing at the sight of them, feeling a love, a connection, a desire that I couldn't put into words.

There's nothing unusual about being a miserable young person. But the source of my misery was more than the usual anxiety about spots, boys and school. Tension over my mother's poor health had set my parents at each other's throats. There was no punching or slapping but the violence of the emotional weather sometimes threatened to break the windows; the general climate was one of hostility and disappointment. I was the essential audience to their big, two-handed drama, involved to such an extent that my daily life away from the house – school, friends, studying – felt as insubstantial as a shadow. None of the normal teenage activities seemed to counter the hefty reality of my parents dismantling each other. The only thing as intense as my experiences inside the house was my deep and absorbing relationship with the landscape, outside.

We lived on a lane near the brow of one of those low, round hills of West Suffolk, amidst fields that stretched over the curves like pegged canvases. The cycle of the farming year painted them with a changing palette of colours and textures – the glossy purple-terracotta of newly ploughed furrows, the fluid, furry lime green of barley ears and the steely metallic jade of wheat. Most of the old hedgerows were long gone, but there were a few wonderful overgrown remains, tangled in bramble and nightshade, and some patches of woodland, with tantalisingly large trees, that spoke of an exciting, more forested, past. From the time we moved there when I was twelve, I was allowed to roam, at will, in all of it.

I would leave the house announcing 'just going for a walk' but what I did was nothing so goal-orientated; I wandered, apparently randomly, between moments of intense looking, listening, feeling, like a dust mote, batted by sights and sounds. I'd crouch down to touch the bent neck of individual cowslip flowers and notice the way the sepals cradled the yellow corolla; I'd turn my head left to right, right to left, repeatedly scanning the way the hills, fields and sky fitted together, as if trying to solve the puzzle of an Escher drawing. I grew obsessed with the shapes of fields. I paced their perimeters, stepping through hedgerows and over ditches entranced by the transition from one space to the next. Some fields felt like an empty stage, ready for the first second of a performance; some like a den or nest; others like the centre of a pentacle where a spell was about to conjure the unexpected. Often I held my breath and often it felt as if time was doing the same.

When I could, I chose portions of the day or night when no one would be about. I took care to place my feet precisely to avoid snapping twigs – I taught myself to make as little sound as possible. My desire was to be invisible, to see and hear and feel without being in any way perceived myself. This was partly because I hoped to see something others would consider exciting – a fox, a deer, a stoat – but also because it helped to summon the wildness that hid in those overworked agricultural spaces. Every square inch of Suffolk has been trodden, cut, trimmed, ploughed, sown and generally interfered with by humans for hundreds of years. Yet out along my favourite green lane, or in the neglected field corner, beyond the wood, there was a sense of remoteness, a dreamlike, otherworldly feel that I've only experienced since on uninhabited islands.

I seldom saw anything that would interest anyone but myself – once a stoat dashing across a lane in bright sun; once the shape of a fox melting into a wood-edge at dusk; once a herd of fallow deer materialising out of a mist in an October dawn. But many times I experienced moments of deep connection with the landscape around me. At these times my veins were open, nature's blood and mine, one system. There are too many times to recount but here are some.

The field opposite my parents' house is a fifteen-acre swoop like a huge wing, from the rounded upper 'coverts' at the hill cusp to the slight concavity formed by the outstretched 'primaries', which run into the ragged hedgerow at the bottom. The far margin is left uncultivated and now, on this still June dusk, oxeye daisies fill the space. I stand amidst the 'chuck-chuck' of partridges as a fat, yellow moon soars over the ghost-pale sweep of flowers, so close I think I can hear the 'shussshhh' of its rising.

I'm up early on a late April morning to catch the moment when the rising sun shines exactly into a cowslip-lined ditch and onto the yellowhammer singing on the wire above. Bird, flowers and sunlight are one thing, as if the song were winding out the gold from the sun to fill first feathers, then the ditch, until they overflow with colour.

A high, clear day in early spring, the land saturated. Wind like a blade and no place to hide from it on the open junction between farm tracks. Blue

is captured in every puddle and a single skylark sings, drawing a small cloud over the land to visit each scrap of water-trapped sky in turn.

I visit a field I have never been to in summer and find my first orchids, common spotted, craning their necks to see over the tall grass. Their small pink heads are balanced on stalks exactly the length of my legs.

I've turned onto a farm track on a winter night, expecting that I'll see enough to be able to walk a well-known route. But I'm stumbling, blind, disorientated, until like a miracle my eyes adapt and I'm seeing, walking, dancing by starlight.

My moon shadow is on the tarmac, like the ideal version of myself, and little owls are splitting the night with their cries whilst, just as quickly, invisible crickets stitch it up again.

Around me, bean-flowers transform the air into a hallucinogenic drug. I sit on the trig point – a little pyramid of concrete that marks the highest point for miles around – and breathe in the scent until I'm flying over the blue-green layers of Suffolk dusk that reach out to the sunset.

I opened my heart and these things were placed there forever. I felt each one, and many more, go in and make its place, too much for words – a completeness that required an outlet – and, since you can't make love to a landscape, I tried to paint.

I carried my moments back to the house, struggling to get their size and weight through the doors, and I took them to my small, dark study, to the sheets of sugar paper and the set of acrylic paints and oil pastels, bought from the local stationers. I tried to capture the subtle shapes of fields, their stage-like openness; I tried to capture the shadows and the puddles and the sky. I tried to make the paint say what was deep inside my heart, to sing the larks and light, the calling partridges and the crickets in the dark.                    »→

Above Wen*nder* Sept 17

Lambedi
9 May 17

But inside the house, these things were slippery as dreams. I couldn't catch them. Every picture failed. Nothing in my marks or colours was recognisable to me. I had no technical skill, no guidance. I wanted abstraction that embodied emotional power; I wanted accuracy that communicated the exact identity of beauty. I stared at work by the painters that I loved – Cézanne, Derain, Nash, Ravilious, Palmer, Constable, Nicholson – and had no idea how to begin on a path that would lead even close to where they were. Perhaps I knew I should sketch, out in the landscape, but I was too shy, too self-conscious to do anything as visible as sit with a pencil and a pad of paper. 'Practice' and 'time' were in another universe, quite separate from me. All I could see in my work were the things I did wrong; I didn't know what mistakes can teach you, about how to like just one square inch of what you've done and learn from the square foot that you hate.

I tore up most of what I painted, with tears and self-loathing. I was defeated, frustrated by the passion that I felt and could not express or share. I decided I could never be the artist that I wanted to be. I tried to be a scientist instead, and by the time I'd mostly failed my parents were gone and all connection with my Suffolk territory was lost. There seemed no way to redeem that lost self or make peace with the dramas of the past.

I understand now that my desire to paint was part of a search for belonging. If I had managed to express my landscape-love through art, would I have felt that I belonged in Suffolk? Through imbibing a place so deeply that it became a part of me, would I have become a part of it again? I don't know. All I know is that I searched for somewhere to belong all my adult life and never found it. Then, three years ago, I moved to a tiny village in the hills of South Wales and fell in love with a landscape again.

Just as if it had been a human love affair, I remember the moment it began: I was trying out a little running route in the lanes around my new house when the view stopped me dead. The curve of the lane disappearing downwards, the bare trees and beyond, the hillside red with bracken, the cone of Sugar Loaf mountain just greening in the early spring light. My heart turned, raced, leaped up and tried to escape from my chest.

*When in love, the sight of the beloved has a completeness which no words and no embrace can match: a completeness which only the act of making love can temporarily accommodate.*

On the way to the station that day, I bought a set of felt-tips that proclaimed themselves to be 'for landscape' and began my journey back to my girlhood ambitions, my journey back to myself and to a home.

In three decades I had hardly drawn or painted, but with the first marks I made in my small notebook, the old, visceral satisfaction of putting line and colour on a white page flooded me. Instantly, the desire to make pictures was compelling. Instead of having the terrible performance anxiety that had filled me when I made pictures as a teenager, I felt deeply at ease. When I looked at what I'd done, I didn't want to destroy it because I recognised something in it. A little of the place but more of the feeling I had experienced when stopped still at that curve of lane, that dip of hill. I saw in my inexpert marks that moment when I had fallen in love.

I also recognised that there were parts of the picture I'd made up, because I couldn't carry them in my head. For the first time I truly understood that I couldn't carry a whole landscape in my eye – I needed to go back and look and, this time, take my sketchbook with me.

I still have no technical skill, no real idea of how to go about painting. The difference now is that somehow I've learned to look. As an adolescent I couldn't get through my own internal storms – my fragile sense of self – to see clearly enough. Now I can put myself aside and turn outwards, not in, and I have found a new joy in picture making.

I have found something else too: a route into the creative part of my brain. My pictures are very definitely not about the non-fiction, poetry or stories that I write and yet the creative space in which I find myself, because of them, helps my writing. As I'm looking and making a picture, my brain enters a kind of dream state where boundaries disappear – I enter story space, that place where real and imagined, old and as yet uninvented, can collide and intertwine. If I'm struggling with a text, sketching helps to clear the knot.

But the most important thing is that finally I have a way to express the growing passion that I feel for the landscape of this Welsh valley – which is truly one of the most beautiful places I have ever known. With every picture, my connection to this place increases. Although the core of me is perhaps too unrooted, too wandering ever to feel I truly belong, I am finding the sense of completeness for which I longed as a teenager. I can be, in a small way, the artist that I wanted to be – and through that I have come home at last.

# THE FLOW COUNTRY

## LAND OF MOUNTAIN AND FLOOD

*Words:* Laura Morgan
*Illustration:* Magi Sinclair

*The Scottish counties of Caithness and Sutherland are home to the world's biggest blanket bog. With a unique blend of species and an expansive language around peat, it is also a place where human history stretches back five thousand years.*

It's late on a January night. The car's headlights pick out a stretch of tar-and-chip road edged by grasses that bleach in the glare. Turning to look out of the passenger window, I see only a half-outline of my face lit by the glow from the dash. The darkness flows out uninterrupted, the landscape absent even of the shadows of houses, trees, farms or hedges.

'Four thousand square kilometres.'

'What is?' my husband asks.

'The bog,' I say.

I'm still looking at the pool of light from our headlamps, where the grey single-track road appears from nothing and disappears again in our wake.

'It's like travelling through a void,' he says.

Snow begins to fall. Large flakes pelt the windscreen but are batted away by the wipers, and soon the road turns white. The lights reveal fluorescent snow poles that mark the edge of the tar-and-chip. In such an open landscape, it only has to snow like this for a short time and the road will disappear from sight.

Satellite images of Scotland at night reveal great constellations of light emitted from Edinburgh and Glasgow in the south, and a trail of dots heading up the east coast to around Aberdeen and Banff. Almost everything north and west of there vanishes into darkness. Some of this darkness is peatland. We're in the county of Sutherland, close to the border of Caithness, and we're driving across what is arguably the world's biggest blanket bog, an area two and a half times the size of Greater

London. Since it first came to the attention of conservationists in the 1950s, this terrain has been known as the Flow Country – 'flow' being a Scots term for a morass, probably from the Old Norse *flói*, meaning marshland. Locally the word is pronounced to rhyme with 'plough' and refers not to the moor itself but to depressions where streams run. Near the sea cliffs, there are countless seams and folds which create these waterways. For the crofters who graze cattle and sheep, the bog, sitting higher than the coastal grasslands, is known as 'the hill'.

At the end of the Pleistocene, some ten thousand years ago, when the ice was retreating, the landscape here was one of plains and smooth hills. Temperatures rose and trees grew – juniper, hazel, birch and willow. When the climate turned wet, peat consumed the trees in a process known as 'paludification': the dry ground became waterlogged and moss took hold. When ground is wet, normal seasonal decay is slowed, causing a deposit of rotting vegetation to form. Such deposits accumulate only under a subtle alchemy of conditions that include poor drainage, cool temperatures, consistent cloud cover and rain. When all these occur, the rate of accumulation exceeds the rate of decomposition. In some places the peat sometimes reaches a depth of ten metres. Unlike raised bog, which usually forms in basins, blanket bogs have no distinct edge, spreading into grasslands and carpeting even steep slopes. Moss and lichen blanket the land.

The Flow Country is home to an unusual blend of species that thrive in its highly acidic, low-nutrient soil: carnivorous sundews trap beetles and flies in their pink sticky hair, and floss-like starbursts of bogbean flowers prick the surface of pools, roots braiding the water. Where moss floats, the morass becomes *sùil-chritheac* – literally 'a trembling eye' in Gaelic. The peat mosses are of the genus *Sphagnum*; although it can be hard to tell them apart, there are at least twenty-five species here. In some the leaves are fluted pyramids and in others baubles, but all are translucent, so that when one species, *S. cuspidatum*, glows lime and pink under the surface water, the effect resembles mingling dye. The bog has pools and hummocks and ridges, so that sketching a cross-section of the surface topography describes a wave, with the hummocks and hollows forming peaks and troughs. In aerial photographs, the land appears textured: islands of dark water shine from the ocean of moss.

There is more blanket bog in Scotland than in any other country in Western Europe. The carbon stored in its peatlands is estimated to be equivalent to a hundred years' worth of human-derived environmental pollution. Disturbing the peat releases this carbon back into the atmosphere. Although much of the Flow Country is now a reserve of the Royal Society for the Protection of Birds (RSPB), some is owned privately by game estates or occupied under crofting tenure. Gamekeepers undertake controlled burnings of the heather to improve habitat for grouse and other species. Crofters dig ditches for drainage and have a legal right to cut peat from designated banks, which they use to fuel, stoves or ranges that heat both their home and water. It can be hard to find a balance between centuries of tradition and conservation, especially when, to many outsiders, the bog is just a wasteland, a nowhere place. In the 1980s, private investors, attracted by tax breaks, afforested large tracts of the flows, an action that lowered the water table, causing the *Sphagnum* moss to die and the bog to shrink back. The RSPB has since bought a lot of this land and is gradually felling the trees, using the trunks to block ditches. The brash, consisting of branches and twigs, is left to rot in the tracks of the harvesting machines. Eventually the bog will claim it.

The peat's high acidity and lack of oxygen preserve everything from pollen to human remains. The peat accumulates at a rate of one millimetre per year, so each metre in depth represents a millennium. Car exhaust particles from the past century press down on ash from the eruption of the Icelandic volcano Hekla in 2300 BC. At the deepest level of the bog are hazelnuts from 5000 BC. Often trunks and roots from the long-consumed forest are uncovered when crofters dig peat from the banks. This bog wood is renowned for burning bright.

........................................

We lost the last radio station signal miles back but we keep the car stereo on at low volume in case a voice returns. Somewhere out there, beyond my half-reflection in the window, is the Flows Lookout, an observation platform built by the Peatlands Partnership in 2015. On days when cloud sits low to the bog, the sight of the cylindrical, larch-clad tower rising from the empty tundra looks like a relic in some distant human-less future.

Tonight I see none of this but sense the land rolling. The now white road stretches into the darkness and I turn again to the window, but all is black, the flakes melted in bog pools. Over time — and the moor has lots of time, having already whiffled away seven thousand years — the peat swells in some places and compresses in others, but always the movement is upwards. The hummocks become hollows, and the hollows hummocks, and the permanent pools — well, they stick around, and in some places these *dubh lochans*, or little black lakes, are big enough to swallow cars.

Sometimes when I'm driving on the coast with the peatlands to the south and the Atlantic to the north, the road feels more like a causeway. This expanse of moor might be the reason the Gaelic language survived here for decades after it was lost elsewhere in the Highlands. Writing in 1980, the academic R. D. Clement noted that remote parts of the mainland 'behaved like islands' in preserving Gaelic culture.

The language of peat – in both Sutherland Gaelic and Caithness Scots – is as expansive as the flows, with words for the lifting, the casting aside, and the stacking, and a detailed vocabulary for the cut pieces. In Caithness, the sod from the top of a peat bank is *tirvin* and poor quality peat is *yarfal*. In Gaelic, a small peat is a *caoran* and the dross is the *smùrach*. There are names for pieces shorn of turf, for ones cut with an ordinary spade instead of a traditional peat spade, for wet peat laid aside, and for the various methods of constructing a stack – round, pyramidal or perhaps four or five pieces placed like a house of cards, which in Sutherland Gaelic is a *storàg*. In 2002, archaeologists found a fossilised pyramidal peat stack in the Outer Hebrides that had been abandoned and consumed by the bog. It had been there, they think, for around three and a half thousand years. So once another language must have given words to the cutting and stacking of peat.

As our car continues along the track, I see a patch of sky in the distance where the darkness is deeper, and I know this is the copse of Scots pine and spruce in the hamlet of Kinbrace. There's a light in the window of an estate cottage, another in the kitchen of a modern bungalow. The trees hide a few other houses. Before the Highland Clearances of the early nineteenth century, the river valleys that cross the peatlands – known as straths – were better populated. Here in Strath Ullie, between 1813 and 1819, more than a thousand people were displaced. The landlord wanted fertile land for large-scale sheep farming, and his factor apportioned strips on the coast to those evicted whilst others boarded ships to Canada. To the west in Strathnaver, the names of lost villages ring like a litany: Ravigill, Rhiphail, Rhiloisk, Rossal, Rhimsdale. There is little left of these places – a tumble of stone under grass and moss, a collapsed gable end and an empty hearth. But standing stones, cairns and brochs (prehistoric circular stone towers) suggest a human history going back five millennia.

For much of this time, peat sustained life here, providing fuel in a treeless landscape. Because kindling was scarce, it was considered bad luck for the fire in a hearth to go out. At night, the flames were *smoored* (a Scots word meaning damped down) with ashes, which allowed the fire to take again when raked in the morning. According to the hymns and incantations recorded by the folklorist Alexander Carmichael during his travels in the Highlands in the late nineteenth century, the *smooring* of the fire was accompanied by a prayer, such as 'The Sacred Three':

> *To save,*
> *To shield,*
> *To surround.*
>
> > *The hearth,*
> > *The house,*
> > *The household.*
>
> *This eve,*
> *This night,*
> *Oh! this eve.*
>
> > *This night,*
> > *And every night,*
> > *Each single night.*
>
> *Amen*

...............................................

In the passenger seat, it is my job to watch the fringes of the road for deer. The red deer, its coat textured like the moor, is Britain's largest wild animal. The males can weigh up to 200 kilograms (around 440 pounds), enough to crumple the front wing of a car on impact. It's easy to think of the red deer as the moor's only inhabitants, but they share the wetlands with lesser-seen roe deer, otters, pine martens and mountain hares. And of course there are the birds. In this brindled and

ochre landscape are several migratory species, which also breed in the Arctic tundra, and here in the far northwest greenshank nest. In summer, black-throated divers swim low on the lochs, golden plover run jaggedly over the peat hags and dunlins call *treep* overhead. Earlier, before the snow fell, we passed what looked like a herd of about thirty red deer at a bend in the road. The sweep of our lights turned the elevated vegetation grey-brown and many pairs of eyes glinted back through the dark. Another snow flurry turns the night to television static and I lean forward in the seat, concentrating more.

I'm not sure what happens first – the light flashing on the dashboard or the slide – but we are suddenly pivoting clockwise. The tyres have no traction in the snow, and as we head away from the grey strip of road into the night, the car feels weightless. The only other movement is from my husband's hands on the steering wheel, frantically turning it anticlockwise. Everything else stops. I brace myself against the seat. Somehow we miss the bog, but now my side of the car is closing in on a snow pole and I'm certain we're going to hit it. The rear straightens just in time and I watch the pole pass close to my door. Looking back it felt like this all took place in silence, but now I remember the radio static and one of us swearing.

'We're ok.'

I breathe.

The snow keeps falling.

At last we see the lights of our village on the coast. The radio whispers, the station returns, though the programme we were listening to when we set out over the bog finished an hour ago.

At home we light a fire. It's late and we should be going to bed but the journey has electrified our minds and limbs. We listen to the kiln-dried pine snap and pop in the grate.

'What about that spin?'

'I swear we just missed the pole.'

I throw another log on the fire, thinking of Carmichael's prayer and the acres of peat to the south of us, the depth of their blackness rolling out under a night sky. *To save, to shield, to surround. This night, and every night, each single night.*

# CROSSING THE THRESHOLD

## CUT LOOSE AND SET ADRIFT

*Words:* Raynor Winn
*Illustration:* Georgie Bennett

*Home is a patch of earth we call our own and a set of surrounding walls that encompass generations of stories. This is a story of what happens when we close the door for the last time and step into the unknown.*

The fields smell of honey in the late evening. They have been managed organically for twenty years and the hay meadows are rich in red clover, vetch, sorrel and buttercups – food for clouds of pollen-drunk bees that lift from the blooms to make their way lazily home. A line of beech trees alive with insect life stretch their long two-hundred-year-old shadows across the land as the sun dips behind the mountains. The sheep, settled on the dry earth beneath, are transfigured in the purple and pink hues of the evening sky. I pass through the lower wet meadows, brushing hands through sedge grasses that hide rare moths and silver-blue dragonflies. Beyond the alders and silver birch where the blackcaps spend their summers, I find the stream, lush with marsh marigolds. The curlews nest in the wetland at its edge, feasting on tiny elvers as they run upstream. They lift from the long grass with startled calls, leaving late-fledged chicks crouched and hidden. I crouch too. At the edge of the water all is silent and, as the light fades, he comes – an old dog fox following his path from the woods out into his own secret world. He stops, wary, drinks from the stream, then bounds across and is gone. For years our paths have crossed, but they never will again. The cold water runs through my fingers downstream, always moving, never still, as I must learn to be.

In darkness I return to the house, no need for a torch – I know each fence, each tree, each mound of earth. I reach the corner and feel my way along the rough granite to the door. The stone walls are three feet thick, built without mortar, stone laid on stone with patches of straw or mud between. To walk through the doorway is to pass through time. A short tunnel from the world of light and action to another space, another era. Running my hands across the stones, the past seeps out in smoke and dryness, the future left outside and the present a blurred space between the two. As the door closes, silence. The hum of nothing. Then a sound that has travelled through time, a constant through the six hundred years that these walls have stood. A faint distant scratch from deep within the stones. A mouse from the present settling for the night on a bed of straw from another age.

So many people have passed through this house, so many have called it home. In 1485 the boulders that form the base of the walls were heaved from the ground and levered into a trench that would form a foundation. They have stayed in that very spot through generations – no need for concrete or metal, they have remained through flood and drought, earthquakes and fires. Hours spent in a dusty records office reveal that we are not alone – the plight that my husband, Moth, and I face has occurred here many times before. These stones are only a temporary shelter.

In 1812 Robert takes his horse into the barn by the house and removes its harness. He's just ploughed the field, preparing to plant the corn that will feed his family and animals for the coming year. He couldn't have ploughed the field without that horse. Without it, he and his wife and three children would have starved. In another world, the Napoleonic Wars rage and William Pitt the Younger has invented income tax. How could Robert have known about wars or taxes, out here at the edge of the land and barely able to read? Darkness descends and he settles his head on his blanket pillow, listening to the deep breathing of his wife and children and to the quiet movement within the walls. Tomorrow he will sow the seeds with hope for the next year. A faint light breaks through the shuttered window and there's a commotion outside. Robert opens the door. He is snatched into the arms of soldiers – ripped through the doorway for not paying taxes and marched thirty miles to the county jail, his horse led alongside, taken as part payment. In the first month of the three years he spends there, his wife and children are evicted. Within six months his wife has died and his children are lost.

Time billows through the house, in smoke pulled by the draft of the opening door. The wide inglenook encloses an open fire that burns with a flickering, jumping flame. The ash logs from the fallen tree are dry and spit with a bright heat. We pull two wooden chairs close to the pool of light; we've turned off the lamps and the darkness of the house falls behind us. Our children sat on stools in front of this fire twenty years ago. Soft little things, eating with tiny, eager fingers. We knew then that beneath the Artex and plasterboard lay another age. So we set it free, let the past out, let it breathe into the future. I lean against the huge granite stones that form the cheek of the inglenook and I can feel it. Time. And Sarah.

It was 1843. Sarah and her husband, John, were outside when the roof fell in. The bracken and heather thatch that held the rain of a wet winter had given way under the downpours of the spring. The landlord had won the house and all the other tiny crog-loft dwellings on the estate in a game of cards. These small houses with a dwelling space beneath a sleeping platform were the homes of tenant farmers. Their livelihoods, their futures and their hopes were lost and won in the turn of a card. John walked twenty miles to plead with the landlord to allow him to take wood from the forest to replace the rafters so that they could support a new thatch. Sarah and their six children made their beds in the barn and waited for him to come home. He came with strange news. The landlord did not want the roof re-thatching. He wanted slates. Slates from the quarry ten miles away. They would be free, but John would have to fetch them himself. He was fifty-one years old and it took eight journeys with his old horse and small cart to collect the slates through wind and rain, across the mountain. He battled against one hundred and sixty miles of Welsh weather and terrain before the family could pitch the new roof. Together they carved '1844' onto the new roof truss before they heaved it into place. All the while a pile of new thatch lay in the barn unused and dry, a bed for mice and dogs. In the winter of 1844, John died on the sleeping platform beneath the new roof. Within the month, Sarah and the children were evicted. What landlord would rent a farm to a woman? A woman couldn't run a farm. In the summer of 1845, the family looked south towards Wales for one last time, as they hung over the handrail of a ship bound for America.

We've protected this house and land, Robert, Sarah and I. It has been our home and we have moved stone and earth to form and shape the landscape around our needs. Our calloused hands and our exhausted minds and bodies are all testament to this. And yet there have been days when each of us has straightened our backs and looked to a blue sky scudded with broken white clouds, as the swallows have swooped through, feeding on the wing. Each of us has put a hand to our eyes to shield them from the sun – and each of us has wondered.

Moth drops another log into the flames, keeping the fire burning as he has for the last twenty years. The granite at my back reflects the heat of the fire and I'm surrounded by warmth. A deep recess in the side of the inglenook forms a bread oven where generations of farmers have raised loaves made from grain grown in the fields. We've stored logs in that dark hole, and warmed lambs that were close to death until the heat brought them back to life. I've sheltered the children in there, when a hurricane broke through the door and threatened to take the roof. But now it's empty, the last of the logs burned. The small, dark form of a mouse drops over the lip of the stones. Following their shapes to the ground, he scurries across the slate floor and is gone. We are alone. Our thread of time here is over. Like Robert and Sarah, the people my research found living here before us, I'm about to cross the threshold of this ancient house for the last time. All of us ripped away by others, not leaving by choice but evicted and powerless to stop it. We sit, as the last embers of the fire dim and the dark stillness folds around us.

Humans have lived without a permanent home for millennia. As hunter-gatherers we have moved across the land sheltering in caves and woodlands or travelling nomadically with tents and livestock across open plains. Only with the advent of agriculture did we stop. When we began to plant crops, we had to be still. No longer needing to move with the food, we had to wait for the crops to grow, wait for the food to come to us. Without the safety of movement, our predators now knew where to find us. Unable to migrate with the changing seasons, we had to adapt our lives to sit out the weather patterns. As we became stationary, a permanent shelter became a basic human need. Was this when we created the concept of home?

The light breaks. A grey dawn. We will shed the life lived within these walls, leave this land. Leave the crops unsown, the hay unmade, the fire unlit, the food uncooked. The walls are silent. Time has stopped. We step into the unknown, into the world beyond the door, beyond the land, beyond home. Robert was taken, locked away from the land. Sarah crossed the sea in hope.  ⟫→

We hoist a few possessions on our backs and head south. We pass swallows who are heading north, but unlike them our destination is uncertain. They have left their winter homes in Africa and travelled thousands of miles to this safer, cooler climate. Free to move with the natural resources, to feast on our insects and shelter their young beneath our eaves, they are drawn by a magnetic thread of knowledge passed through time. Nomads of the air, settling back into their northern home. People eagerly await these heralds of summer, which bring a filigree of swooping movement to a fixed place.

We head south to walk a path that we do not know, across a land we have never visited. I am mourning the loss of my land. A farmer's daughter formed by the land, I'm defined by a close connection to my patch of earth, by the rhythm of seasons, of sowing and reaping, by knowing the smell of the soil, the pull of the grass to the sun and being one with it. But, as I pass through this unknown land and lose these markers of time and place, I feel my sense of connection to nature slip out of reach and with it the knowledge of who I am. I can no longer hear the sounds of the walls. I am cut loose, set adrift without anchor or rudder.

We walk into a land of cliffs and gulls, following the edge of a sea that stretches away to the south coast of Wales. My home and my sense of what home is become distant, separated from me by a wide stretch of water, yet home still feels so close I could almost reach out and touch it. I crave the safety of its enclosure, but I tear my eyes away and fix them instead on the South West Coast Path, allowing its magnetic pull to take me forward. Exposed to wind, rain and burning sun, we walk on, our only shelter the tent we carry. The same wind, the same sun, but without my land I am disconnected, just walking through weather systems. As I crouch on a beach of smooth sea-worn stones and gritty sand, a flock of turnstones mill around me, scratching and peeping until the light fades and they head away into the night. As the flicker of a driftwood fire rises into the air, I can only see the sparks and hear the sound of the sea lapping on the rocks. I am lost, but the draw of the path strengthens me and we keep moving forward. We share mornings in dewy grass meadows with thousands of ladybirds hatching into their first flight, and dusk with badgers tracking food as the moon rises over the sea in shards of silver crystal light. I look north for the lights along the Welsh coast, but they have slipped from view. All trace of home is gone – there is only the path.

The age of mankind's simple nomadic existence left little evidence of wars or extreme violence. At a time when people followed their food and the weather, there was little to fight over. When the food was gone, they moved on, allowing the land to recover and regenerate. Our fear of the nomad, the traveller, the tramp, the migrant became deep-seated when we became settled. As instinctive as the need for shelter and food is the desire to protect it – to guard our resources against those who live by consuming what they need and then moving on. Centuries ago, we guarded our grasslands against the transient herdsmen who allowed their animals to graze and then left without helping to build a fence or shoe a horse. Now we guard our communities against those who live outside them, those who live without permanence and threaten our view of pristine locality or property value. But perhaps what we really protect ourselves from is something else – a shadow at the edge of our vision, an elusive echo from the past, a question that irritates our thoughts.

We walk on, caught between the human world and the endless horizon of the sea, through a strip of wilderness as the domestic slips from us. Homelessness has made us nomadic; we are reverting to an older way of being – through need, not choice. We swim amongst dolphins in deep, syrup-smooth seas and float with gulls as they sleep on the water. We pick limpets from shells and chew on bitter seaweeds as hunger takes hold. An ancient battered landscape of rocks and crashing waves crushes our spirit and then holds it up for us to ask why. In the darkness of a howling gale, the wind roars with force and purpose and I am caught by it. The uncontrollable wild strength of the storm finds me. Inhabiting the elements, I come to understand that I don't need to own a piece of land, or to know it with the intimacy of my own skin. I am the land, the sea, the sky, the dry dust and the call of the oystercatcher. It is all one and I am one with it. The land that forms the deepest part of who I am will always be mine – I don't need to possess it to make it so. I am released, regained, bonds rebound. I am held up.

We stand on blocky granite cliffs at the edge of the Atlantic and we are alone – the wide expanse of sea ahead and nothing behind. Just as we removed the Artex from the walls of the house, so the walls have been removed from us. Layers have been peeled back revealing the true form beneath, and we are free. Free to exist, free to choose, free to merely be as we have never been before. I am what Robert, Sarah and I saw when we shielded our eyes against the sun and wondered. My existence questions every day worked, every plough pushed, every animal raised. Now I understand. I am the shadow just out of sight, I am the mouse in the wall, I am the thread of time that makes us a species not a nation. I am what we all are – human, in basic human form, the natural human state that has become strange and foreign and a threat to the settled way of living. A threat to our acceptance of how we inhabit the land and in what form. A threat to our peace of mind.

The 'salt path' leads on to the most southerly point. I stand on the cliff with my face to the wind as thousands of swallows mass, waiting for that perfect moment when their tiny bodies will give themselves over to instinct and spread their wings to head south. I began my journey believing that I would never know home again – I thought that home was a piece of land I owned and a set of stone walls surrounding me, both now lost forever. But I have come to understand that home is no more than a concept, a state of mind, something that offers safety and security. I give myself over to instinct. Letting my eyes return to the path, I follow Moth's footprints in the dust. Home already. ✖

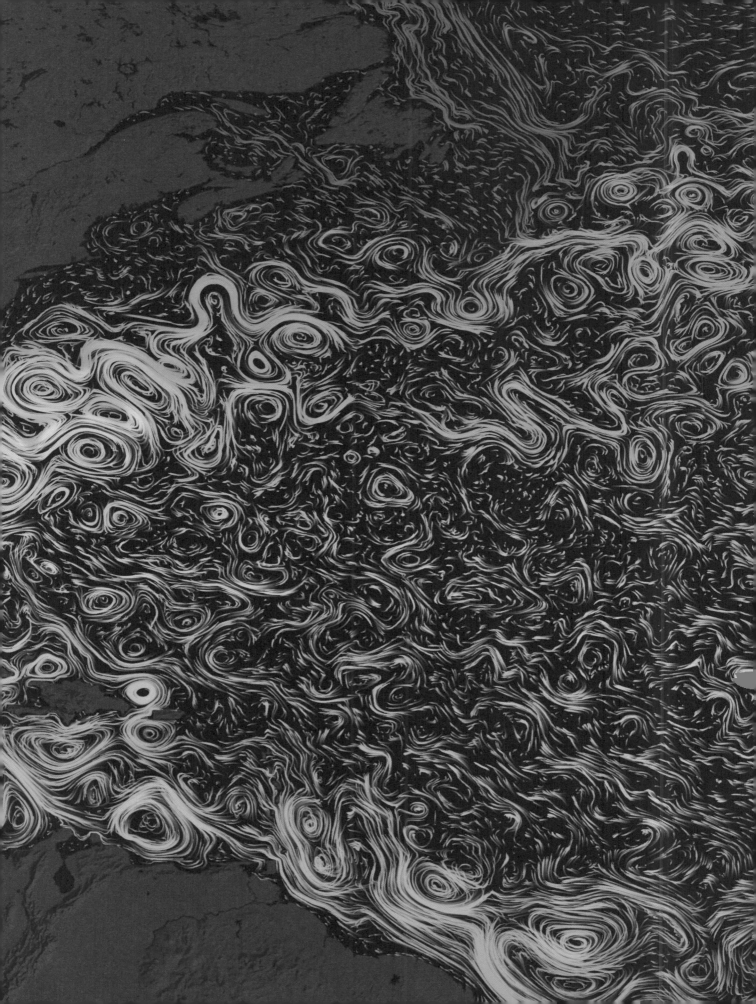

# OCEAN PATHS

---

## WEAVING FROM COAST TO COAST

*Words:* Helen Scales
*Imagery:* Goddard Space Flight Center

*On maps oceans are named and bounded, whereas in truth they are all one body of water. Seventy years ago, marine biologist and author Rachel Carson wrote of their hidden pathways. Now, a lifelong follower of her work is caught in the ocean flow as she traces Carson's life and follows a trail of eels to a wild coast she can call home.*

In the summer of 1949, American marine biologist and writer Rachel Carson went to sea for ten days. It was the first time she had left the coast to explore beyond the horizon. Like it does for all mariners, her world shrank to the size of the ship, in her case a trawler converted into a research vessel called *Albatross III*. Her seascape was drawn in ever closer by dense fog that wrapped the ship day after day. There were visitors to this white, encircling universe: petrels that flew through, appearing on one side and then disappearing like sorcerers on the other, and fish, starfish, urchins, sponges, crabs and lobsters – a sprawling grab trawled up and brought on deck, offering a glimpse of what lay far below. Unseen were great currents of cold and warm water, pressing together over the shallows of Georges Bank and creating a wide curtain of condensation in the air above. The meeting of ocean-borne waterways off America's North Atlantic coast, a hundred miles due east of Cape Cod, makes this one of the foggiest places on the planet.

Seventy years later and two thousand miles away as the petrel flies, I found myself inside a similar cocoon of fog. By then, after more than a week on a ship named after another seabird, the *Pelican*, I had grown accustomed to this floating microcosm where twenty-one people ate, slept and worked. I was used to my windowless state room, a fancy term for the cramped four-bunk sleeping quarters. It had become normal to me that floors were covered in grey plastic with non-slip dots, that I stepped over high lips in doorways and clutched tight to the sturdy metal bar in the bathroom to keep steady in three-metre waves.

Now and then, I climbed up on deck for fresh air and to look for passing dolphins and flying fish. On clear days, the view stretched out around me as a circle of dark, indigo sea. Sometimes there were drilling rigs perched in the distance, sucking oil from deep below like giant, metal mosquitoes. But that day I went outside and the view was hidden. The ship was muffled in fog, tucked inside a small white compartment with soft, gauzy walls so close I might have reached out and touched them if my arms were just a little longer and I wasn't worried about falling in.

As I stood on deck, I remembered how Carson had described her time at sea on *Albatross III*, hemmed in by fog. Surrounded by the same scene, I felt her leaning through the decades and standing next to me.

Carson's work was partly responsible for me being on that ship. Between 1941 and 1955, she wrote a trilogy of ocean books — *Under the Sea Wind*, *The Sea Around Us* and *The Edge of the Sea* — that years ago filled my mind with places I wanted to see and things I wanted to know about the seas and the creatures that live within them. However, those aren't the books for which she's best remembered. More people can name *Silent Spring*, with its potent exposé of the chemical industry, whose pesticides devastate wildlife on land. Her ocean books spoke more loudly to me, or perhaps I chose to listen more intently. Her words helped to push me gently, and without my knowing, into winding currents that would lead me to becoming a marine biologist and diver around the world.

Along the coast of West Africa, in Senegal and The Gambia, I've visited fishing communities and met people whose lives depend on the updraft of food, delivered by a flow that rushes like a waterfall in reverse. Dissolved nourishment rises up and feeds animals in shallower seas — the sole and mackerel that swim offshore and millions of oysters in the mangrove forests, glued to trunks dipped in the edges of the sea. Other currents stir a riot of fish around tiny islands in the north-western Pacific. In Palau, I dived over and over in one particular spot where the current is so strong it's hard to swim against. Rather than use up all my energy and air, I clipped myself to the reef with a two-metre line and hovered like a kite in a strong breeze, surrounded by small, bright butterflyfish and surgeonfish that came to nip at microscopic plankton, and the other bigger fish, the tuna and sharks, that came to eat them.

Another time, in Fiji, I swam in a current that, more than any other that I'd experienced, seemed to want to take me with it. I was diving on a coral reef that had been hit by a cyclone which swept through the islands a few months earlier — the most severe tropical cyclone on record in the southern hemisphere. During my visit, the hundred-mile-an-hour winds had died but still a powerful underwater wind was blowing, not a direct consequence but a memory perhaps of the winds that had been there before. Currents and winds are connected above and below the waterline. Both are stirrings of rising particles of water and air, heated by the sun and sent swirling by the spinning earth. As they blow, winds catch against the sea's surface, tugging water with them.

Down below on the reef, a group of us drifted along the face of a steep, sunken cliff that the cyclone had scraped bare of corals and other animals. I felt like I was flying over an empty, lunar terrain. As the cliff flattened out, I gradually realised my dive buddy and I had become separated from the group and were drifting off on our own. A beat later and I noticed the crosswind had turned. Now it was dragging the pair of us downwards and offshore. Kicks made little difference – it was like running on a treadmill. In open water there is nothing to grab hold of, no reef to cling to. Metres ticked by on my dive watch as we were pulled further down – fifteen, twenty, twenty-five. Panic was rising on my friend's face and I realised it was up to me to get us out of there alive. I grabbed her hands and squeezed. 'Watch me,' I motioned – two fingers to her eyes, then mine. Only two things mattered: go up and don't lose sight of the reef. A puff of air in my dive jacket for added lift. A firm grasp on my friend's hands. Then I kicked and kicked, looked and kicked, taking us away from the deepening, darkening water. Slowly, details began to appear in the outline of the reef – the welcome shapes of corals and tall sponges, the flickering shoals of fish easily able to master this formidable current. Normally, when all is calm, it is so easy to believe I belong here, floating in a magical realm. But occasionally nature sends a warning sign, telling me to take care and respect her tumultuous whims, because really I am just a visitor – a human pretending to be a fish.

In *The Sea Around Us*, Carson writes of how the oceans are connected. No separate mass of water makes up the Pacific, the Atlantic or the Indian Ocean. 'It is by the deep, hidden currents that the oceans are made one.' I rode those currents to many places and eventually reached a point at which I wanted to tell people about this underwater world, to share it in words. I wrote about the oceans, about the sea-shells and seahorses and other animals that fascinate me most. Then I went to live at sea for a while, like Carson did, to gather ideas for a new book about a place I'd never been.

Going to sea was not easy for Carson. At the time, she was editor-in-chief of publications at the US Fish and Wildlife Service and was reporting on studies aimed at understanding why fish in the Northwest Atlantic were becoming harder to catch. These were early signs of the great emptying of the oceans that continues today. To know more about what was being done to decipher these changes, Carson needed to go to sea with the scientists. A previous trip had been cancelled, apparently to the relief of the chief scientist, who later admitted his crew would have resented having a woman aboard. Carson waited a year and eventually a second trip went ahead, on which she was accompanied by her friend and literary agent, Marie Rodell, who planned to write an article called 'I was a Chaperone on a Fishing Boat', much to Carson's amusement. Carson and Rodell grew accustomed to life on the ship and were slowly accepted by the crew. Together, they staved off seasickness, swallowed down the dreadful food and learned to sleep through the clamour of trawling activities that went on through the nights.

In contrast, arranging my voyage was simple. A scientist friend of mine was planning a trip to the Gulf of Mexico. I asked whether I could come along and he said yes, and assigned me a bunk on board. I filled in a medical form, booked a flight to Louisiana, packed two weeks' worth of seasickness tablets and explained to my family and friends that just because it was called a research 'cruise' did not mean there would be a pool on deck and cocktails at sunset. But it was no great chore being at sea. The food was always delicious and the on-board entertainment was spellbinding, if deep-sea biology is your thing.

Mine will be a very different book from Carson's, containing things she never knew. Now scientists can see all the way to the bottom of the deepest seas. Some climb inside cramped miniature submarines and go there in person, peering out of small portholes. On my trip to sea, we took the safer and more common option of sending remote-controlled robots in our place. Each day the crew would winch a car-sized contraption over the side of the ship and lower it down on a long metal cable. Meanwhile, the rest of us lined up in front of computer screens, watching live footage of the scene unfolding two thousand metres beneath our feet: a white squid hovering still for a moment, staring into the camera before jetting gracefully out of view; a purple sea cucumber wafting past, beating a frilly skirt like a flamenco dancer; a giant isopod crawling over the seabed like a land-living woodlouse only a thousand times bigger. How I wish Carson could have seen the things we saw. Not trawled-up animals, damaged and dead, but living and swimming, doing what they do in the deep.

During quieter moments on board the *Pelican*, lying in my bunk, I thought about another place that had recently started to draw me in. The sensible way to get there would be to fly and drive, but if I had the time I could drift and ride the currents that link here and there. I could follow the path of eels that are heading for our mutual destination further east.

Maps trace my route, showing where surface waters swirl and lick across the oceans. There are few clear boundaries and no banks to be seen on either side of these huge saltwater rivers. But scientists have learned to track their paths, using satellites and underwater sensors to measure the wind, the temperature and the shifting height of the sea. All these data are fed into computer models that draw lines across the oceans' restless skin – as particles of water move, they create torrential highways, weaving ribbons and turning circles that spin and suck others into their vortices. Our technology reveals what the eels have known for millions of years. They have minute biological programmes stowed inside them at birth, giving them navigational abilities that mostly remain a mystery to us humans. All we really know is that they have no chance to practise and no time to learn, but still they find their way.

Carson wrote about these eels in her first book, *Under the Sea Wind*. She described their meeting place out in the Atlantic in the Sargasso Sea, where, as she writes, 'old eels were to die and become sea again'. Adults of two species – European and American – mingle there but they do not interbreed. Instead, they find mates of their own kind and leave behind eggs that hatch into transparent, leaf-shaped motes. Each new eel somehow knows where its parents came from and how to get home.

From my spot in the Gulf of Mexico, I could join the beginning of the Gulf Stream, which would take me through a gap between Cuba and the southern tip of Florida. There I would meet the flotilla of young eels. Together we could all head north with Bermuda to our right. Some of them would seek a coast sooner than the rest and steer westwards, perhaps to Cape Cod and the place where Carson spent her first summer next to the sea. For six weeks in 1929, she worked at the Marine Biological Laboratory in Woods Hole. There she studied fish, learned to swim in the sea and began to think of the books she would one day write.

Other eels would carry on further north, their eyes now dark spots and their bodies stretching into thin bootlace versions of the adults they'll become. On the shores of Southport Island, Maine, some would reach the place where in 1953 Carson moved to a cottage she called Silverledges. From the windows she could see the waters of Sheepscot Bay and a short walk took her to a sandy beach and a rocky shore. Here she wrote *The Edge of the Sea*. She collected animals and seaweed from tide pools and brought them to her cottage to study under a microscope. Then, each night, she carefully took them all back to the spots where she found them. In 1964, after she died of cancer in her fifties, some of Carson's ashes were scattered in these waters.

Some young eels would decide to drift in the main flow of the Gulf Stream for a much longer journey. Following them would take me away from Carson's coast and onto a meandering route east across the Atlantic, to a place I hope to call home. Bearing right, I would choose the outermost branch of the current and follow the eels to arrive eventually on the coast of France in a region known as Finistère – Land's End.

There was a moment when I knew I had found somewhere I wanted to stay. It was the first time we had been to Finistère together, my husband and I, and on that day we were looking for a particular west-facing beach, noted for its surfable waves. We had got lost driving along tiny lanes and been given directions by an elderly French lady and her son, after helping them to push their car out of a grassy ditch. We found the beach, parked and walked a short way across heathland, yellow with gorse and pink with heather. And then we stood — silent and astonished — looking down on perfect lines of teal-coloured waves crumbling towards a stretch of sand overlooked on each side by gigantic cliffs, twisted and shaped by time.

Ours was not just a search for waves. So far, we had both spent much of our lives roaming the world, first alone and then often, after we met, together. And we both had begun to feel an urge to stay in one wild space, to put ourselves there and get to know it. We had planned a month-long camping trip to see Europe's Atlantic coast and work out where that place might be. But here we were, at the very start of our trip, and we both knew we had already found it.

Six months later, we came back to check whether our hunch was right. We hiked the clifftops, explored the forests, searched the rock pools and did our best to take it all in. Every day this place worked its way deeper into our minds until there was no chance it would let us get away. Another six months and we were back again. It took just five days of looking before we found the precise spot that we would begin to call our own: a small stone cottage tucked away in its own woodland. From here, paths lead in all directions to the sea. Ten minutes south by foot and we are high on the clifftops, where someone keeps bees that forage in the heather. Thirty minutes in the other direction, along a sunken holloway, lies a cove lined with fossil-filled cliffs that slice through ancient rocks – Ordovician, Silurian and Devonian. Another route brings us to a sheltered bay where pipefish take cover in seaweed and sea urchins chew the rocks and turn them into honeycomb. Walk a little further and we reach a point where the land is all behind us and in front of us, on the opposite side of the Atlantic, is the coast where Carson lived.

Whenever we are able, we are here. And when I'm away I write lists and dream of the things I will do here. I will learn the names of all the shells that wash up on the beaches and all the trees and plants that grow in our woodland – the lichens and the emerald velvet mosses. I will know the birds by the songs they sing. I will wait expectantly for the day when a fire salamander, like a tiny black and yellow dragon, walks past. I will learn how to read the tides and currents that swirl around these, the wildest seas of the region. And I will watch out for the young eels, *les civelles* as locals call them, which have come a long way to be here, as I have, with plans to stay for a while.

# THE CALL OF
# THE DOMESTICATED

## TAMING THE WILD

*Words:* Colin Taylor
*Illustration:* Lucy Eldridge

*One laid-back afternoon on the shores of the Indian Ocean, a pack of humans is adopted by a tropical beach stray. So begins a telling of the age-old tale in which bonds develop when lives human, canine and feline intertwine.*

### STRETCH

One summer I co-adopted a fish-scavenging tropical beach dog – not an exotic and little-known pedigree but a stray mongrel, covered in mange. She turned up, out of the blue, one hot afternoon. At that time, I lived in a surf shack on the Mauritian coast with a Canadian artist called Roxy who studied and painted cetaceans. Our Indian Ocean home was a pale-cream single-storey clapboard affair with a tin roof painted terracotta that had been built in the 1950s. It was loud in the rain, hot in the sun and fashioned to withstand cyclones. The shack sat low and welcoming on a dusty bougainvillea- and tree-lined avenue leading from a coral-sand beach. We named it Sod Hall, an address that reflected our sense of purpose. It was 1992 and we had few responsibilities beyond feeding ourselves. This glorious state, free from responsibility, lasted for the whole of the summer.

Each afternoon we'd play Van Morrison on repeat and the music netted and drew in salty, sunburned and thirsty beach bums – local Mauritians, a jumble of surfers from France, Australia and South Africa… and an equally genetically diverse pack of dogs. They all made their way from the hot beach, heads lolling, in search of cooler, breezy places. The surfers squatted in our yard on dusty breeze blocks in the shade of a broad-boughed Indian almond tree and the dogs lay in the dirt at our feet, panting with dry tongues and occasionally snapping at lazy flies. The surfers were parched from hours spent at the back of the surf, their backs the colour of teak, their bellies less so. The dogs, their coats matted and sun-bleached, had scavenged the tide-line since dawn. We gave our beach strays bottles of Blue Marlin beer and bowls of water, which they gulped down and lapped up gratefully. In return, they gave us their company. The surfers talked into the cool of the dusk about jobs they had dropped, ground swells they had chased, breaks they had caught at reefs from South Africa to Sydney. Some of them sported heroic wounds where late exits from waves had flung their bodies against sharp coral. These healed to pale scars, testimony for the rest of their lives to their blind pursuit of hedonism. Roxy would ask them about the pods of spinner dolphins they'd seen beyond the breakers at the reef's edge, and the beach dogs begged for the scraps we tossed to them as we chatted and drank.

The most regular of all our visitors, human or hound, was a dainty, tan-coloured, short-haired, dingo-looking bitch with comical swept-forward, floppy, pink piggy ears. She would crawl on her belly under the chain-link fence into the yard and approach our group slowly and respectfully. Stopping just short of the porch, she would extend her front legs and arch her back as if asking to be permitted access to the circle. She never assumed. This dog read us well – her perfect manners meant she was welcomed without question and, having won herself the name Stretch, she adopted us.

Strays often had short lives in the tropics at this time as, for fear of disease and attack, they were chased away from homes and beaten savagely when caught. As a result, they were often timid or aggressive, depending on what character trait made their survival more likely. Stretch was different. She was self-assured and walked with her head held high, though not in a lofty manner. She was savvy, but deferential to humans. She already had responsibilities, frequently arriving with the same sidekick stray, who was a less lovable scraggy, black and white tagalong with worse mange and even less personable attributes. We called him Piss Off as it allowed for economy of language when we needed to shoo him away from the yard. Stretch remained loyal to Piss Off even though he was not allowed in the house. Her fidelity to the underdog only served to endear her to us more. We took her to a local vet and he cured her mange, and Piss Off's too so she didn't get re-infected.

Stretch was a unique character – never needy but obedient – and she could have easily become reliant on us but seemingly chose not to. We gave her a blue collar, which contrasted nicely with her tan-orange coat, and it appeared to us that she wore this among the other strays with an element of pride. I'm sure it gave her a higher status among the pack. The collar held a little brass vial in which we placed a note for the dog catcher so that Stretch could be returned to us and spared euthanasia if caught. We resolved that we were prepared to take any fine coming our way to bail her out of the dog pound. The note contained our details and a brief history of our care, explaining that we had rid her of disease and fed her. The note doubled up as a communication to persons unknown, perhaps another household should she have an alter ego.

Stretch and Piss Off would regularly take themselves off on Walkabout into the boondocks for days or weeks at a time. When she was gone we would worry about her and pine for her to return, but she would always turn up again, sometimes with and sometimes without Piss Off, guided to our home by the beacon of Van Morrison and wanting scraps and a bowl of fresh water. With not a little fear of disappointment, we would check the brass vial each time she returned to see whether it contained a response from a different custodian. To our relief there was never another note so, happily, after

a while we concluded that we were her only human family. To us this meant she had no other name and listened to no other music. One day Piss Off did not return with Stretch. We never saw him again. Thereafter, Stretch spent longer periods of time with us and less time in the bush. She had lost her charge and we were her new responsibility.

Eventually our summer came to an end. Roxy's and my future plans were uncertain but involved going our separate ways and leaving Mauritius. We had decided that we couldn't bear to leave Stretch to fend for herself even though she would have been more than capable of doing so. We felt that she had invested so much emotional intelligence in domesticating us to her needs that she deserved recognition and reward for her efforts. However, we had to decide which of us was going to take responsibility for her. Roxy was heading back to a home in Wyoming – about as far from the sea as it is imaginable for dog or human to be, and a strange location for both a whale expert and a piscivorous canine – and I had to return to the UK to find work. Stretch and Roxy had a special bond, however, and I think the language between them was more fluent than anything I could manage. So Roxy was Stretch's chosen one.

We had to raise funds to fly the dog back from the Indian Ocean to the United States, so I sold my surfboard to one of the breeze-block surfers to fund part of the cost and a whip-round among her salty friends made up the rest. We held a leaving party and barbecued the tuna we had caught earlier in the day when returning from a whale-study trip. The surfers came dressed in drag, drank the place dry and slept where they collapsed.

Stretch took her first and only long-haul flight in her stride and in Wyoming swapped the beach for prairie seamlessly. I missed both Stretch and Roxy, and in 1994 I made a trip out to the States from the UK to see them. Roxy had to attend a conference on whales in Galveston, Texas, so we took a road trip from Wyoming to Texas and back in an old Dodge pick-up. We covered 1,600 miles south in two weeks then 1,600 north along the feet of the Rockies, taking Stretch to the very edge of the Grand Canyon just outside Flagstaff, Arizona. We camped in the wild, sleeping in the covered cargo bed of the truck, parking up at the many state parks along the route of the Goodnight–Loving Trail, a north–south route where cattlemen had herded their steers to market a hundred years before I was born. When the trip was over and the autumn snow started drifting in the northern states, I said my goodbyes to them both and flew home.

We were both ready and prepared to take on new responsibilities – Stretch had taught us that. I embarked on a new profession and married, and Roxy found love with a rancher and specialised in 'big country' art. Stretch learned a life around horses and cattle, roaming free of a lead all her days. The tropical beach dog discovered the delights of playing in thick drifts of snow and snoozing in the warmth of wood fires. She lived out her time hopping in and out of pick-ups and barking at rattlesnakes and grizzly bears at Painted Creek in the shadow of Yellowstone National Park. Stretch, the mangy beach stray, lived for nine years after flying to the United States, leading a life she would not have seen had she not tamed us. She bound us together and gave us more than we gave her – and for that we are indebted to that stray dog.

Sod Hall? The termites chewed it over decades and it finally blew down in a storm. Fittingly perhaps, the spot where it stood is now a surf school where life's untroubled sup beers while perched on bricks, hanging out with the dogs.

## FOX

It was some years later and, as is the way with many things, my life had changed to one of employment, family and responsibility. I found solitude and time to reflect while working on our allotment, digging a small plot of stony ground and making efforts to grow food for the family plate. There, one late spring evening while forking up early potatoes, I became aware that I was being watched. Circumscribing the perimeter of the allotment, about fifty yards away, was a young male fox. His nose was down and sniffing, and his tail bushy. He was clearly checking me out – most likely curious to see what I was doing and whether it might afford a chance of food.

Eagerly hoping to prolong this human–fox interaction, I took care not to spook the wild creature. I continued to dig and weed, slowly and predictably, speaking quiet encouragement in a low, non-threatening tone. My manner seemed to have the desired effect and incrementally the fox drew nearer. At ten feet it stopped, faced me and sat on its haunches, ears pricked up, stiff and alert, twitching independently at each peep or rustle of bird noise from the bushes around us. I straightened up, turned to face it and calmly leaned on my fork. We stared at each other. A deep gaze, eye to eye, into the inky-dark privacy of each other's pupils – no embarrassment or awkwardness at the intrusion into personal space. I wondered what it saw in me – friend or foe, food or a cause for flight. The moment was, for me, amazing. I felt wonder and privilege at the trust this animal was showing me. This was not a city fox habitualised to human contact – we were in the countryside, deep in fox-hunting territory. This animal had every reason to be wary of me.

Slowly, slowly I crouched and extended my arm to the fox. It did not start or run away but stood, maintaining eye contact, and with hesitant steps came within touching distance. I reached the back of my hand further forwards. It pushed its muzzle towards me and I felt the cold, wet tip of its liquorice-black nose touch my knuckle. Since the Palaeolithic, when we began to separate ourselves from other animals' ways of living, a few humans have been allowed such flashes of contact with wild nature, and it was a moment I will never forget. It lasted for a minute or so more before my rufous friend turned away from me and casually sauntered off, vanishing into the obscurity of a copse at the edge of the allotment. This close encounter of the canine kind left me wondering why it had moved me so. I had not felt the same way about other encounters with wild birds, fish or small mammals. There had been something fundamentally different about meeting the fox. Perhaps unromantically, I struggled to believe something spiritual had happened. There had to be a less poetic explanation.

It seems there probably was such an explanation, and it was all about the gaze. A study led by Miho Nagasawa and published in 2015 showed that gazing into another's eyes increases a human's oxytocin levels. Oxytocin, the 'love hormone', is produced when people cuddle up, bond socially or gaze wondrously into another's eyes. When Mr Fox had me look into his eyes, a chemically hypnotic interaction essentially got me loved up. Nagasawa and colleagues also determined that when they sniffed oxytocin, dogs increased their gazing behaviours. Oxytocin is excreted in urine, of which there would have been plenty around prehistoric human settlements. From this I interpreted that dogs and humans seemed destined to become enamoured with each other's company – a special bond arising from a quirk of chemistry.

Indeed, we have been chemically bound to hounds in Europe for aeons. Dogs were domesticated around a hundred thousand years ago and certainly before the last great ice age. Fossil remains from caves in France show that humans and dogs were living together twenty-six thousand years ago, and studies have shown that modern wild foxes can be domesticated in just eight generations. (Interestingly, the price a fox pays for adapting to a human environment is less starch in its ears. Whereas wild foxes have pricked ears, domesticated foxes' ears are floppy, a trait also typical in domestic dogs.) I hoped I'd see the dog fox again but I never did. He was wild, and I was fragrance free and of no benefit to him. The love was all one way.

My hormonal fox-fix faded, and I returned home with a pitiful crop of thumbnail-sized potatoes and a few slug-ravished lettuces. At this time I was part of a family of five, one of which was an elderly cat. There is less evidence to show that cats have a chemical effect on humans, but I contend that cats are more advanced than that – they operate on a more psychological front to subjugate us.

## MOWGLI

Eight millennia ago, cats first curled up with humans in warm corners across Turkey and Cyprus. They were tens of thousands of years behind domesticated dogs, but since then they have caught up decisively. I wonder whether they peered from the fringes of the forest and observed how dogs, with the loss only of a little dignity and pricked ears, had made a beneficial pact with humans. African wildcats, determined to cut a less exhausting deal and no doubt unimpressed with the prospect of hunting with humans or goofing around chasing sticks, devised the passably helpful domestic ruse of catching vermin. Like cunning door-to-door salespeople, this got them a paw over the threshold of our dwellings and access to snug fur rugs from which they could scheme for greater survival advantages. Like the opportunists we know them to be, felines inveigled their way into a succession of pharaohs' hearts, becoming venerated as gods and sealing the deal as bona fide household occupants. Thereafter, the human world was theirs for the taking and they spread across the globe.

Cats have also flirted with fame, taunting us with their superpower of having multiple lives. Oskar was rescued from the sinking of the German battleship *Bismarck* by British sailors aboard HMS *Cossack* during World War II. When that vessel was sunk by the Germans, he was rescued for a second time and boarded HMS *Ark Royal*. Dispensing with yet another life, he was hauled from the water 'angry but quite unharmed' when the *Ark Royal* was torpedoed. Three lives down, Oskar went into retirement in Gibraltar and then spent his final days in a manor house in the English countryside.

Later, in 1963, a female cat accepting of the name Félicette became the first of her kind to venture into space, no doubt on the understanding that she would be brought back to Earth alive, unlike her hapless canine predecessor, Laika.

For some time, too, cats fixated on famous men named Ernest or similar. Mrs Chippy explored opportunities for her feline kind in the Antarctic, taking Ernest Shackleton with her. Snowball encouraged Ernest Hemingway to write prose about fish. A cheeky anonymous cameo from a white Persian cat sat in a position of command upon the lap of James Bond's arch-nemesis, Ernst Blofeld, gave us a glimpse of its kind's dubious intentions. Tabby and Dixie took this ambition beyond fiction to infiltrate the most powerful office in the world as Abraham Lincoln's companions. Ludovic le Cruel impressed Cardinal Richelieu with his cunning. Mark Twain could barely string a sentence together without the comfort of Bambino, and Choupette Lagerfeld inspired Karl to create all manner of haute couture. Whether their stories are well known or not, many people have fallen for the allure of cats and in so doing further cemented them into the collective psyche of our lives.

The scheming, the quiet air of contempt, the keeping of odd hours, the mood swings, and the courting of the famous and influential – I put to you that cats are clearly the ultimate organised crime group of the Animal Kingdom. Whereas dogs have sealed their place in history as our best buddies, we proverbially kiss the signet rings of cats. It is not yet clear what their nefarious purpose is, but it is the case that organised crime groups also seek to include law enforcement in their sphere of influence. And so it was that I met Mowgli.

Some years after my encounter with the fox on my allotment, my profession as a police officer took me to St Mary's, the largest of the Isles of Scilly, where I was the senior officer for the archipelago. I was responsible for law enforcement and headed up a small team that included the station cat, Mowgli. Like a mogul, he required a door attendant in order to be let in or out according to his whim, as a cat flap could not be installed due to security. We would often find ourselves sipping black coffee or green tea while his lordship lapped up the last of the milk from his bowl on the floor. At team briefings one of us would have to stand as Mowgli lay asleep on one of the chairs. He was of indeterminate age but he displayed distinctly elderly feline habits – he slept, he ate (noisily) and then he slept again, rarely acknowledging our existence.

For several years my small team of four and I coexisted at our tiny police station happily, oblivious to the inconvenience of every chair being felted with Russian Blue cat hair. It played havoc with our black uniforms and we ran out of parcel tape regularly as copious amounts were used to pat each other's posteriors clean before we could venture smartly out of the station. It got everywhere, and was a peerless practical demonstration of cross-contamination and of the forensics maxim that every contact leaves a trace.

I struggled initially to find a benefit to having a police station cat. He was also of no entertainment value and there were no small vermin for Mowgli to keep in check. Nor was there any prospect of a cat sniffing out evidence or catching a fleeing suspect. Instead, my policing team on the Isles of Scilly became subservient to an animal who inconvenienced us, displaced us and took liberties with our hospitality. But advantages did emerge, and they were numerous and unexpected.

One of the most bureaucratically feared events in the life of a copper is a visit from Her Majesty's Inspectorate of Constabulary (HMIC). A jostle of senior-ranking officers will descend on a police station with as much warning as one may get for an earthquake or tidal wave. These are infrequent events but potentially devastating when the report is written up. I received just such a visit on St Mary's.

Flying into the islands for a custody inspection were a superintendent and a chief inspector. I was informed of their impending arrival by phone only about fifteen minutes before they landed. This was the late morning of my day off, and I just about had time to steer my boat safely back to harbour, moor up and race the hundred yards up the hill to the police station to meet my two smartly uniformed, serious-faced inquisitors as they disembarked from the airport taxi. The established rule when meeting a senior officer is to salute them if both of you are wearing a hat. Therefore, to avoid awkwardness, the unwritten rule is never to meet a hatted senior officer if you are not yourself wearing a hat. Having just disembarked from my boat in a Hot Tuna T-shirt and beige cargo shorts, I had no option but to extend a hand to the most senior officer and introduce myself as the police sergeant for the islands. As she shook my hand, we both realised that my hand and forearm were splattered in dried blood. I knew this to be from my haul of mackerel, caught earlier that morning, but what the inspection team made of it I wearily presumed would form the basis of section 1.0 of their St Mary's Police Custody Improvement Plan. The only passable expression in such an instance is a sheepish smile. I showed the officers into the police station and offered them a seat and cup of tea after their long journey. I washed off the blood and knocked the sand off my flip-flops while the kettle boiled. They looked at the bowl of milk on the floor next to them and then back up at me with disdain as I handed them black tea with a hopeful shrug and a second sheepish smile.

The inspection commenced, and at the conclusion I was asked rhetorically, 'Can we see your cells now?' Nothing is denied an HMIC inspector. I pushed open the unlocked door to Cell 1 and they peered in. I had no doubt that it would pass muster as it had been renovated to Home Office standards several months before and used only once since. I stood back to await their inevitable non-committal grunts of acknowledgement but instead a gasp from the superintendent surprised me. I looked into the bare concrete room to see both of them closing in on Mowgli, who was curled up, one indignant eye open at the sudden intrusion. As they leaned over him, clipboards under their arms, the one in charge looked back at me over her shoulder. Resigned to my fate, I exhausted my day's quotas of sheepish smiles.

'Ooo! He's a lovely chap isn't he? Can I pick him up? What's his name? I've got two cats. My neighbour is looking after them while I'm away. He's so big! What breed is he?'

You are either a cat person or a dog person, and this superintendent was most certainly the former. The rest of the inspection went without a hitch. With much fussing over Mowgli, who deigned to get up and take a supercilious sip of his milk, the mood relaxed. The pens were clicked back onto their clipboards, which were returned to briefcases, and I was invited to regale the visitors with stories of our feline colleague. They were most heartened to learn that when our latest prisoner had been booked into custody, his specific request, after receiving his rights, had been to meet the station cat rather than contact a relative or solicitor. It was opined that having a cat about the place was a marvellous idea for team welfare. As the inspection drew to a close, we had a last cup of black coffee each and they made their goodbyes to Mowgli before leaving for the airport. I followed them out of the police station front door, noticing that the seats of their uniforms were covered in fine cat hair.

Mowgli went on to become a firm favourite with the team, with the wider community on the Scilly Isles and especially on social media. A picture of Mowgli with a brief diary entry on his sedentary escapades always went viral, attracting the attention of thousands of fans all around the globe. Even the city of Olathe in Kansas covered the story of when I found a goldfish unceremoniously dumped on the doorstep of the station. 'Goldfishgate', as it came to be known, was never owned up to but the main suspect was Mowgli. Tourists specifically called in at the station just to see our big cat, and on a visit to the islands the local police and crime commissioner made a beeline for a photo opportunity with the Russian Blue, nearly putting his back out lifting him. Later another fan, the deputy chief constable, gave Mowgli his epaulettes and promoted him to the very same rank in an honorary capacity. Both officers left the station wearing Mowgli's fluffy-trousered badge of honour.

History will record whether or not cats are part of an organised crime group. In due course one may emerge from their ranks to be a leader. But it will not be Mowgli. He has retired now to a pool of sun in the country. What their demands will be when they have us firmly under their influence is not clear. It may be for our total annihilation but somehow I doubt that. I rather suspect that the inevitable Feline Rights Act will include just three articles:

The right to unfettered access to any home.

The right to a warm, undisturbed place to sleep.

The right to a fresh bowl of milk.

# FROM THE HEART
# OF THE TREE

---

## FIRE SEEKER

*Words:* Wyl Menmuir
*Illustration:* Neil Gower

"Grant me your hidden fire,
Oh, Banyan tree
Speak a prayer to the Banyan tree,
Kindle a fire in the dust
Of the Banyan tree"

*The theft of fire from the gods is a thread that runs through the fabric of myths and legends worldwide. From Prometheus to Azazel, Nanabozho to Crow, theft and trickery are inextricably linked with our acquisition of fire, a secret so valuable that deities and gods wanted to keep it for themselves. The prevalence of these stories is hardly surprising — the taming of fire for cooking, for surviving the cold, for farming and industry allowed nothing less than the transformation of human life. Fire brings us together, and we have told some of our greatest stories around the flames.*

*In Polynesian legend, stories of Māui, the shape-shifting trickster demigod who could take on various forms including a pigeon and a lizard, appear on islands as far spread as Hawai'i, New Zealand, Tahiti and Tonga. In some Māori retellings, as well as raising islands from the sea and lengthening the days by ensnaring the sun, Māui was responsible for tricking the fire goddess, Mahuika, into revealing the secret of fire.*

In the time before tales were told around the fire while the fish cooked, for there was no fire around which to tell the tale or over which to cook the fish, the goddess Mahuika, in a rare fit of benevolence, gifted the villagers at the foot of her lava field a single flame and then returned to the underworld deep beneath the scorched mountain. For fear of facing the anger of Mahuika, whose sister was Hine-nui-te-pō, goddess of death, the villagers kept their fires burning constantly from that time onwards.

One night, while the village slept, the young demigod Māui sat by his fire, mesmerised by the flames, and wondered where the fire came from. He could hear the answer his father had given him as a young boy – 'From the embers of last night's fire' – but this answer no longer satisfied him. The question lodged itself into his head and would not leave him be. Unable to sleep, he rose and with great care doused his parents' fire. Then he went from house to house, hut to hut, cave to cave and extinguished every fire. For the first time they could remember, the villagers awoke cold.

He smiled as he listened from his bed as the news spread.

'How will we cook our food?'

'How will we stay warm at night?'

'How can we live without fire?'

The villagers ran from house to house looking for embers but each hearth was cold.

'There is only one option,' said the keeper of stories. 'One of us must seek out the goddess Mahuika and fall upon her mercy. Once, her mountain home itself burned and the smoke of her fires filled the sky. Her fingernails are seeds of flame and though she guards them closely, if we beg her she may help us as she helped us once before.'

'No one has seen Mahuika in an age,' one man said. 'Her mountain is cold and if she is even still there, she is blind and infirm. It will be a matter of minutes to take her fire from her. If I did not have aching joints, I would do it myself.'

One by one, the villagers made their excuses until only Māui was left.

'Mahuika is my grandmother,' he said. 'She will not deny me this request.'

Māui travelled across the lava fields until he came up against the sheer face of the scorched mountain, where he spoke a karakia: 'Rock, I am Māui – open to me'. The mountainside split and a tunnel opened. The air inside the mountain was sulphurous and thick, the tunnels dark, and he walked blindly, following the growing heat to its source.

When the heat was becoming unbearable, a whisper began to bounce off the walls of the tunnel.

'Who disturbs my long sleep? Come closer.'

Māui followed the whisper and emerged into a great hollow beneath the mountain. Mahuika rose before him. Her body glowed, a patchwork of shifting colours – white, blue, violet, white – and from the tips of her long fingers sprang flames.

'Grandmother, it is me, Māui,' he said and shielded himself from her heat. 'The fires in the village have gone out. I have come to ask you on behalf of the villagers for some more fire.'

'Grandson, you must tell the villagers to be more careful,' she said, and as she talked she pulled off the smallest of her fingernails and handed it to him.

Māui carried the burning nail away from the volcano, though the further from the mountain he got, the more he began to wonder what would happen if all of Mahuika's fires were extinguished. What would happen to the world? Where would fire be found then? When he came to a stream, he dropped the fingernail into it and watched as it hissed and spat and as the ember faded, and he returned to the scorched mountain.

'Mahuika, I am a clumsy demigod and a terrible grandson,' he said when he returned to the mountain. He shrugged as teenagers shrug and held out his hand. 'You have nine fingernails left – surely you can spare me one more?'

With some anger, Mahuika tore off another of her fingernails and when Māui returned again, empty-handed and full of contrition, having dropped that nail into the stream too, she gave him another. He repeated this process, apologising for the fate of each burning nail, until he had taken all but one. When Māui asked for the final nail, Mahuika plucked it from her hand and instead of handing it to him, she threw it to the ground. The air itself filled with fire and as Māui ran, the flames followed him through the scorched mountain tunnels. When he came to the vent, he turned himself into the form of an eagle and flew up into the air. Lava erupted from the mountain and singed his feathers and all around fire blazed, earth burned and waters boiled.

High in the air above the burning ground, Māui called to his ancestors Tāwhirimātea, the god of the weather, and Whaitiri, the goddess of thunder.

'Grandmother has set fire to the land,' he said. 'Send rain. Send a flood.'

Rain poured from the skies and doused the flames. With his eagle's eyes, Māui watched as with the last of her breath Mahuika blew the final dying spark into the heart of the trees, where the water could not reach it.

When the waters subsided, he wandered among the trees and eventually he found fire, hidden in the dry sticks beneath the banyan tree. He found traces of it too hidden within the dried branches of the fig and the lemon hibiscus, and he gathered an armful of the dry wood and brought it back to the village. There he showed the villagers how to release the fire within to cook their food and keep themselves warm, and around which to tell the story of how he, Māui, had brought fire back to the village.

Later, while the villagers told stories around the fire and cooked their fish, Māui's mother said to him quietly, 'You have been lucky. You have humiliated the gods of weather and thunder and angered the goddess of fire and escaped with only singed feathers. You may not be so lucky next time.'

And Māui laughed, as cocky youths do, and avoided his mother's glare, staring instead, mesmerised into the flames.

# FORGING STEEL

## AN ANCIENT ALCHEMY

*Words:* Monica Coyne
*Photography:* Jay Armstrong

*Carbon and iron are two of the most common elements in the universe. They are in all of us, in almost everything we see, and they make steel, one of humankind's most important yet destructive innovations. In the forest of Humboldt County, a blacksmith strives to find lessons in shaping molten metal.*

## APRON

My apron is a thick pigskin. The light-brown leather is stained black with coal dust and the oil that comes off new steel and rust. This creates a sheen decorated with lines and shapes that are randomly burned into the leather as I use the apron to shield myself from the hot metal. When iron and steel are heated to a forgeable temperature, a thin layer of iron oxide forms on the surface. When struck with a hammer, the red-hot scale pops off and will stick to and burn right through any skin it lands on. The apron is heavier than it looks and notably warmer than the cold steel tools and equipment. Leather is never really cold like steel. The apron is comfortable, like a second skin. Protection from the heat. Protection from the cold.

## SHOCK AND AWE

I first took a job as a metal fabricator in 2003 when the news was full of the rage and destruction spilling out across the world between my country (the US) and Iraq. Metalwork comes with a measure of violence. The metal stock is heavy and sharp. It is either uncomfortably cold or dangerously hot. The air is often filled with caustic dust, smoke or flying sparks. Projectiles are common in a metal workshop. Working in this environment helped me to redirect the anger I felt at the choices my country was making. My husband's cousin had been killed in the attack on the World Trade Center and this was not the response we wanted. I put on my apron, earmuffs, dust mask and safety glasses, put my head down and went to work.

## COLLABORATING WITH STEEL

Before I began to work with steel, I worked with other materials. When I worked with clay, I had complete control over the material. I could push it with my hands and smooth it with my fingers. When I worked with wood, I was at the mercy of the rigidity of the material. I could not push it around. I could only cut it and carve it. Forging steel is like forming clay, except that steel is much tougher and hotter. I have to make tools to shape it. It has its own agenda. This allows me to be a collaborator with the steel itself. I can move it with a hammer and tools, but the steel always surprises me. As the hot material cools, some of it will move, some will stay in place. This trait makes it the medium perfect for depicting figures. It stretches like skin. It folds and swells like muscle and fat.

We are controlled by our perceptions. Innovation and depredation have propelled us forwards as a species. But our greatest strength is our ability to talk each other into things. Humans have an amazing ability to morph and control the way they see the world. My work is an experiment in altering my own perception of what a bar of steel represents. Can I push this metal around in such a way that when I see it, I see a human figure? How much change do I have to make to the material before I start to believe? How little can I change the bar yet still change my perception? Steel is common and inexpensive. Steel is a great conductor. Often, we only notice it when it is too cold or too hot. We notice that it is hard and heavy. Mild steel is either black or rusting and often seen as creepy. Pushing back against the macabre character of the medium, I want to talk the viewer into seeing the beauty of it. As I design, I balance steel's heavy presence with space. Moving it from the outside and then from the inside. I watch the steel's reaction to certain processes. I listen and try to understand the inherent properties of the material and what it wants to say. As I push it, I push myself and the craft out of its box. My movements become more complex and I begin to see things differently. This broadens the possibilities of form that the steel can take, which, in turn again change my perception. I follow the shape and feel of the manufactured form through the piece and out the other side. We grow and change together.　　　　　　　　　　»→

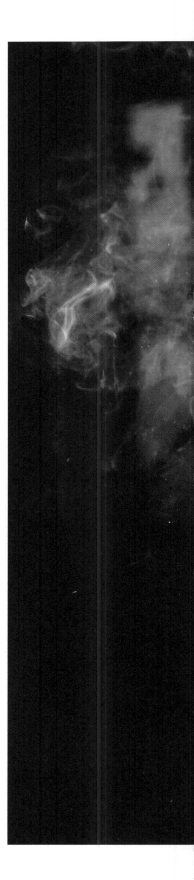

## FIRE

Fire is a natural force but, unlike earth, water or air, it is not a state of matter. Instead fire is a side effect of matter changing form. I use fire in my forge to change wood into charcoal and coke into heat. The heat softens the steel so that I can move it. Without fire there would be no steel. There would be no pottery. There would be no warmth in my wood stove.

I have lived in the forest in California for thirty-three years. The weather has changed here. The winter rains used to be spread out from mid-October to April and sometimes May, but the summer is pushing back and is now hotter and longer. When I first came here, when my children were growing, we never packed them up and fled because of a weather warning. There were fires but the humidity of the long winters and the continuity of the deep forest slowed them down. Our species is changing the atmosphere. We have cut down almost all of the old-growth trees. This leaves us with forests of second growth. Younger forests that have had their large ancestors removed do not have the fire resistance of a healthy forest.

Red Flag Warnings are issued when warm temperatures, low humidity and wind combine to create a high danger of fire. They are being issued more and more often. Fire is a reaction. It is a force of nature that reacts to changing conditions. We are feeding it.

## COAL

The sharp smell of coal is not so different from the tangy, wet smell of leaves and dirt and banana slugs. Every day I walk on a path from my house up a small rise to my metal workshop. Large tanoaks lean towards and away from the building. Madrones bend and reach towards each other. The workshop is nestled in a hollow created by a steep hillside and towering trees. I step from one environment into the other. The damp cold of the forest is softer somehow than the cold of the metal tools and cement. Using kindling from the trees outside, I start the fire. The wood turns to charcoal. The pile of coal begins to burn, sending up thick ringlets of smoke that form lazy, whimsical shapes before they are suddenly sucked up the flue. Put steel into a fire and a transformation happens. The metal changes colour. The atoms vibrate and shift from one pattern to another, adjusting their bonds to each other as the temperature changes. The air seems to contract as the steel heats up and softens. The tone of the fire drops as the metal reaches a yellow heat. Inside the workshop and outside in the forest, there is order and pattern. There are atoms and elements moving and changing – aligning themselves for some unknown purpose.

As a blacksmith I get to play with the elements. But there are rules: I am not allowed to touch the two-thousand-degree steel. I have to extend my senses to the ends of my tools. And I can only work within a limited temperature range, which restricts the amount of time I have to move the steel. It is a kind of dance. The rhythm of the hammer and the blacksmith alternating back and forth from the fire to the anvil.

The trees above my workshop strain against the wind. The sound is deafening. My body tenses as the wind whips through the forge and blows out the pilot on my blowtorch. Leaves and branches rattle and break. I feel myself and the trees relax as we listen to the invisible force comb out along the canyon. We brace for the next gust but then become calm when the first drops begin to fall and the storm progresses from rage to sorrow and release.

## THE FORGE BRINGS UP QUESTIONS

I stand in front of a pile of coal and watch the metal as it is transformed from red to orange to yellow. There is a connection to other humans who have done this for thousands of years. Those people were also fascinated by this medium. I think about what they did with it. Where it led. Where it is leading.

Steel is made of iron and carbon. Iron is the sixth most abundant element in the Milky Way and the fourth most common element on Earth. It is in my blood. I know what it tastes like. Without iron, my blood would not carry oxygen. But I exhale carbon. Carbon is the building block for most of the molecules that maintain life. No element is more essential to life than carbon.

The more we study ourselves and the world around us, the more we learn how similar we are to our environment. Iron and carbon are shape shifters. They are two of the most common elements in the universe and they are in us. Put together they make steel. Ancient humans burned wood and made charcoal. Charcoal is carbon. They heated rocks that contained iron and discovered that when the iron ore and carbon mixed it made a highly usable metal. Humans have a deep connection to steel, and our relationship with it has been both ingenious and complicit. ⟫⟶

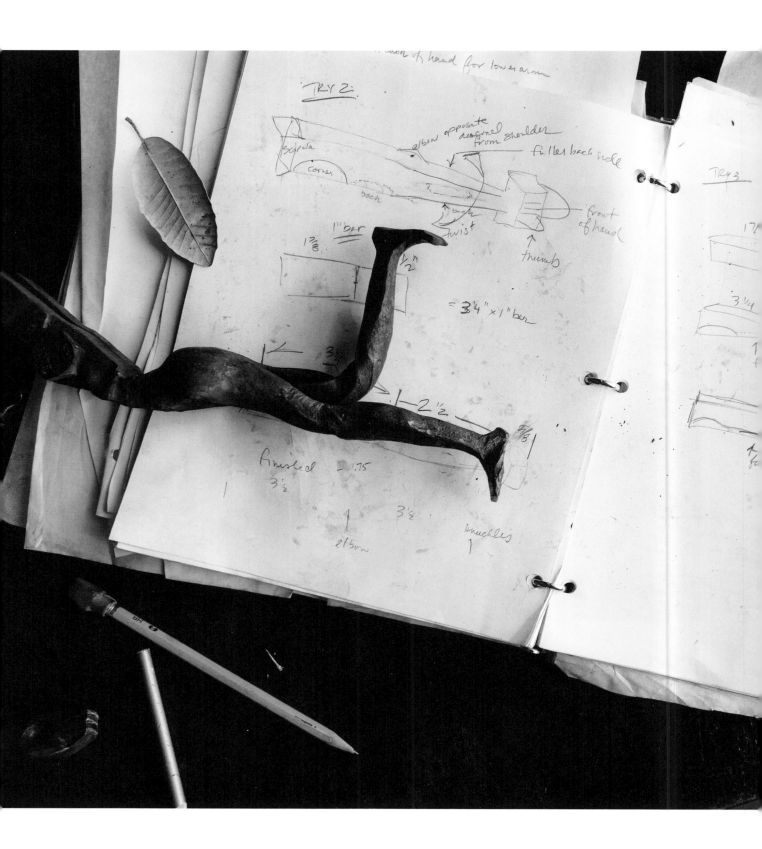

The process of making usable iron is one of humankind's most important innovations. There is evidence that it was a fundamental step in our evolution as toolmakers. But there is also overwhelming evidence that we are now doing irreparable damage with the skills we have learned. There have been five mass extinctions on Earth in the past 500 million years. We are in the middle of, and are accelerating, the sixth mass extinction. It is happening much more rapidly than the others and hinges on our manipulation of carbon. The very same ingenuity that has allowed us to turn a lump of iron into a skyscraper or a plane or a bomb is also responsible for the rapidly expanding extinction of over a thousand other species, the overheating of the atmosphere and the acidification of the oceans.

I am trained in industrial arts and have been a professional blacksmith for fifteen years. I work with iron and steel all day long. I worry about my carbon footprint. I burn coal and propane. I get a lot of steel from scrapyards but when I need new steel, I do buy it. I try to mitigate that by living off grid. I use solar and hydro power. I have an oxygen generator for the propane torch that is powered by the sun. These things do help, but I know that mitigation is only a justification to do what I want. I know I am complicit. But working with this medium somehow makes me feel hopeful. This mixture of carbon and iron, this ancient alchemy, lights up my mind like nothing else. I could quit but the rest of the world will keep pushing forwards. Perhaps I can create a discussion about our choices. So often we give up the wild around us to pursue our progress. Can we instead use our ingenuity to have both?

LOOKING FOR ANSWERS

I live in rural Humboldt County in northern California. My house is on a dirt road and when you go outside you are standing on soil or rocks or grass and looking at trees. I grew up in San Francisco, but my kids grew up in the country. When my daughter was about two and a half years old, we visited grandma in the city. We went out to the corner store. As we walked hand in hand down the street, my daughter looked up at me and asked, 'Are we outside?'　　➤➤

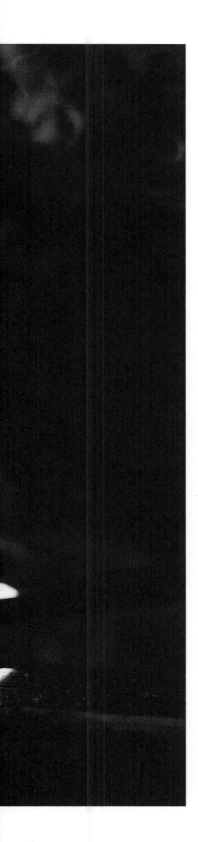

Are we outside? That is such a good question and it has dogged me ever since that day. How do we fit into this world? We have been here a while. We have been drawing pictures and making sculptures for more than fifty thousand years. That gives us occupancy of this place. We are supposed to be here. The cement on the city sidewalk is just as natural as the haystack of wooden sticks that makes up the woodrats' nest behind my garden shed. I know. I know this sounds like an excuse for all of the shitty stuff that we have done and keep doing. That is not my intent. For goodness' sake, because of us, now even the dusky-footed woodrat is in trouble. But I need to explore this connection. Everything here on Earth is made from the same building blocks. We can manipulate the elements, but everything is constant. We are part of a closed system. These building blocks can help us to see a way forward. Listen.

People always tell me that I am lucky to have found a passion. I agree. I love what I do. I am driven to do it by some strange force within myself. This force propels me like nothing else I have ever experienced. And I wonder whether it is just a drive – a common human drive to manipulate the environment. When people say 'passion', they are indicating that the thing they love to do is something natural and wild. Something not solely driven by the human brain. I understand this idea of passion. Sometimes when I am in my workshop, I can feel it. Like an untamed life form, I collect sustenance by way of observation and experience. And then sometimes, deliberately or by chance, I produce sculpture just like a tree produces fruit.

The news is still bad. Even worse than when I started. But I'm still here with my apron, safety glasses and earplugs on, pushing the metal around, trying to understand.

# MIGRATIONS

INVISIBLE THREADS

*Words:* Stephen Moss
*Illustration:* Jenny McLaren

*Migrations remain one of the natural world's greatest phenomena. Watching house martins glide and soar above his village in the west of England, a naturalist contemplates the aerial voyagers that connect us to one another across the globe.*

On warm summer days, when I'm in my garden on the Somerset Levels, I often hear the sounds of two birds – one a rather tuneless chirping, the other a more melodious twitter. These sounds are made by the only two British species named after the place where they – and I – live: the house sparrow and the house martin.

Both birds, as their names suggest, breed in or on human dwellings – a habit widely recognised in other European languages too. Names for the house sparrow include the Dutch *huismus* and the French *moineau domestique*, while the species' scientific name is *Passer domesticus*. The house martin is *huiszwaluw* in Dutch, while in French it rejoices in the splendid name *hirondelle de fenêtre* – 'window swallow'.

Every time I leave my home, I hear the strangely comforting sound of the house sparrows that build their nests beneath the eaves. And from April to August, I see house martins flying above the village, along with swallows and the occasional swift. While house martins do not nest on my home, there are still a few down the road, flying in and out of their neat, cup-shaped nests made out of tiny pellets of mud.

The wildlife TV presenter Bill Oddie points out that house martins bear a striking resemblance to miniature killer whales. It's not just their blue-black and white coloration but also the way they cruise through sea-blue skies, remorselessly hunting down their prey. Another observer, Theunis Piersma (author of a delightful monograph on the species, *Guests of Summer*), draws the conclusion that both the whales' and the martins' contrasting dark upperparts and white underparts may have evolved to confuse their prey. Certainly, as I watch house martins hunting in the clear April skies, uttering that gentle *prritt* call, I can appreciate the resemblance.

Yet, although the house martin and house sparrow share this space with one another for half the year, in autumn and winter they could hardly be further apart – both geographically and in terms of their behaviour. House sparrows are quite literally 'home birds', which throughout their short lives rarely venture more than a minimal distance from their birthplace. House martins, conversely, are global voyagers. Along with the swift, the cuckoo and a couple of dozen songbird species, they head south for the winter, crossing Western Europe, the Mediterranean Sea and the Sahara Desert to reach equatorial Africa.

And then they get lost. Well, not exactly lost – their inbuilt navigational systems mean they know where they are, and more importantly how to return in the spring. But we have no idea where they spend the winter. Astonishingly, even though we have placed small metal rings on the legs of more than four hundred thousand house martins since bird-ringing began more than a century ago, only a handful of these birds have ever been found south of the Sahara. Up to fifty million European house martins simply disappear every autumn. Although we may soon find out where they go by fitting them with tiny transmitters, this currently remains one of the greatest of all natural mysteries.

Migration fascinates people more than any other subject connected to the natural world and gives rise to all sorts of questions. The first – and one I am often asked – is why birds such as the house martin bother to migrate at all. Given the many hazards they face on their biannual journey – notably bad weather and predators – why would they risk their lives to travel so far, instead of staying put on familiar ground?

In the case of the house martin, the answer is obvious. Like all members of the swallow family, they feed on aerial plankton: tiny flying insects, virtually invisible to the human eye,

which they snatch out of the ether. Occasionally, they chatter frantically to warn their fellow feeders that a predator – usually a hobby or sparrowhawk – is approaching.

But as the chill winds of autumn begin to blow and temperatures drop, flying insects disappear. If house martins did not migrate away from their summer breeding grounds, they would soon starve to death. House sparrows, on the other hand, are seed-eaters, so are guaranteed a regular supply of food all year round.

This all seems to make sense. But it doesn't tell us why some birds that feed on insects gleaned from foliage or crevices in trees – such as the treecreeper, wren and goldcrest – stay put while others – notably most warblers – migrate. This may be a question of size: wrens, goldcrests and treecreepers can exploit ecological niches that even slightly larger birds cannot, and so have a better chance of surviving the cold weather.

It is often said that long-distance migrants 'choose' to head south for the winter, but it's not quite as straightforward as that. These species do not choose to migrate any more than their sedentary relatives decide to stay – both strategies are the result of aeons of evolutionary development, which has led some to become migrants and others not.

Another thing that often puzzles people is how birds that spend the winter in Africa know when to return. The answer is that their brains have evolved to be sensitive to tiny changes in the amount of daylight. In the tropics, the variation in day length is nothing like so pronounced as in the temperate regions, but even so the birds are able to detect the shifting seasons.

At a certain point each year – around the time of the spring equinox in the northern hemisphere – migratory birds are able to perceive the small reductions in the amount of daylight south of the Equator. They respond by starting to head north, back to where they were born. To them, this is a biological imperative, but for me, anxiously awaiting their annual return, it marks the moment when winter imperceptibly starts to shift into spring and my home patch comes to life once again.

But spring is coming earlier and earlier with each year. Changes to the earth's climate mean that birds can no longer rely on their long-established patterns. Some are benefiting from these changes. Resident species – especially those like the blackbird that raise two, three or even more broods in each nesting season – can take advantage of the milder weather and greater availability of food and start nesting earlier than usual. Although a sudden cold snap may cause their first attempt to fail, on balance the gamble is probably worthwhile.

Likewise, for the great tit, which feeds its young on the abundant caterpillars of moths, being able to vary the start of its breeding cycle is essential, as in early springs the moth caterpillars may emerge several weeks before their expected date.

But for long-distance migrants such as the pied flycatcher, which also feeds its young on moth caterpillars, there is no such option. Because their return is triggered by variations in daylight, which remain constant from year to year regardless of the weather and climate, these birds tend to arrive back at roughly the same time each spring.

In the past that worked to the birds' advantage, as it gave them time to defend a territory, find a mate, lay eggs and hatch chicks to coincide with the annual glut of caterpillars. But nowadays, with springs coming earlier than the long-term average, they may find that by the time they have chicks in the nest, the food supply on which they rely is no longer available.

Might they evolve to deal with the new equilibrium? There is natural variation within each bird population, meaning that some members of each species always arrive a little earlier than others. If spring does come sooner in a certain year, those early birds will, on average, raise more young than the latecomers, and so pass on the tendency to migrate early to their offspring. This might mean that enough individuals of a species will adapt and survive, preventing their extinction. But it is by no means certain that this adaptation will happen quickly enough to prevent widespread population decline.

The final question I often hear is, 'Why don't swallows, house martins and other migratory birds remain in Africa instead of travelling all the way back to temperate regions?' When I first visited Masai Mara National Reserve in Kenya twenty years ago, I soon discovered the answer. During that trip I saw no fewer than ten species of swallow and martin, from the familiar sand martin to the more exotic mosque and rufous-chested swallow and the gorgeous white-headed saw-wing.

Most of these species breed in Africa, staying there throughout the year. But a few, including the house martin, have evolved to spend the northern summer in Europe. There, they can take advantage of the longer hours of daylight and reduced competition for food, and can raise their families before heading back south again in autumn. The further north a bird goes, the more it is able to take advantage of long days, more food and fewer rivals.

This also brings into question the popular assumption that these birds are 'British'. In what sense is the cuckoo a British bird, given that the male may only spend a couple of months here before heading back to its African home? Likewise the nightingale and the swift: given that these birds spend the majority of their lives away from the British Isles – travelling, like the house martin, to sub-Saharan Africa – what claim can those north of the equator make on them? Some might also argue that the cultural resonance of these species, celebrated for centuries in verse, song and folklore, outweighs the brevity of their sojourn.

So far, I have only talked of birds: the most visible and best-known of all wild creatures, whose presence – or absence – at different seasons of the year is easy to observe and measure.

But many other flying species also migrate, sometimes in vast numbers. One Sunday in July 1508, the chronicler Richard Turpyn recorded how the people of Calais were stunned to see 'an innumerable swarme of whit buttarflyes… so thicke as flakes of snowe'. This was one of the first recorded observations of the little-known phenomenon of the mass migration of butterflies. A few years earlier, on his second voyage to the Americas, the explorer Christopher Columbus recorded a similar swarm near the island of Cuba – the earliest known account of the migration of the monarch butterfly.

Closer to home, 2009 saw one of the greatest natural events ever witnessed in Britain: the invasion of the painted ladies. During the course of that spring and summer, countless swarms of these attractive butterflies reached the island's shores.

I remember sitting in my garden on one sunny Friday afternoon, at the end of May 2009, and seeing a large, long-winged butterfly racing through on its way north. A moment later there was another, and then another. They were not stopping, and at first I was puzzled, wondering whether my usual butterflies – small tortoiseshells and peacocks – had suddenly and inexplicably changed their behaviour.

Then, I managed to get a close enough look at one as it whizzed past, and finally realised its identity. It was a painted lady – an elegant vision of orange, white and black – and a butterfly I usually only see once or twice every year.

That was just the start. Soon, they were everywhere, outnumbering all of the other familiar butterflies put together. By the end of that incredible year, it was estimated that there may have been as many as a billion of these colourful insects across the British Isles, from the Isles of Scilly in the south to the Shetland Isles in the north.

The painted ladies had travelled all the way from Spain and North Africa. And, like the red admiral (a much more common sight in British gardens each summer), they had flown well over a thousand miles to reach north-western Europe. Little over a century ago the Victorian entomologist Edward Newman was ridiculed for suggesting that butterflies could travel across the English Channel from the continent, but the exceptional invasion of 2009 firmly planted the idea of migrating butterflies into the public consciousness.

But painted ladies are not the only migratory insects to reach this country. The following year, I was idly gazing at peacock butterflies feeding greedily on the nectar of a buddleia bush when a different movement caught my eye. For a moment I was completely baffled, as a large, brownish-coloured insect hovered right in front of me, moving rapidly from bloom to bloom as if late for an urgent appointment.

It took a few moments for my bewilderment to clear and for my brain to catch up with what I was seeing. So strong an impression did this make on me that I later wrote about it. I was looking at a hummingbird hawk-moth.

> *Finally, the realisation of what I am looking at begins to dawn.*
> *The synapses click into place, and I feel my face crack into a smile.*
> *For this vision of beauty whizzing back and forth before my eyes*
> *is none other than a hummingbird hawk-moth.*

If any one moment sums up for me the true miracle of migration, this is it. I knew that this species – whose appearance and behaviour so resemble that of a genuine hummingbird that many observers believe that is what they have seen – had travelled all the way from North Africa to be there in my Somerset garden. Like the swallows twittering overhead, it felt as if an invisible connection had been created between me and the rest of the world, a sentiment articulated so well by Ted Hughes in his poem about the return of swifts, in which he notes that their annual return indicates that 'the globe's still working'.

The annual arrival of disparate creatures – from cuckoos to house martins and from hummingbird hawk-moths to migrant hawker dragonflies – travelling across the surface of the earth to my little corner of the West Country is not exactly a miracle in the true meaning of that word. Yet, in the vernacular sense, it is exactly that, filling me with joy, wonder and gratitude for the incredible workings of the natural world.

But we must surely wonder for how long we will be able to celebrate the wild creatures that live around us. Ironically, in this rapidly changing world, some of the commonest and most familiar species – both migratory and sedentary ones – are the ones most at risk.

In Britain, house sparrow numbers are plummeting at a rate of almost fifty individuals every hour, and since 1966 there has been a loss of a shocking twenty million sparrows – a bird once so common it was taken for granted. This decline is likely to be due to a combination of factors. One is a loss of nest sites, because modern buildings have fewer nooks and crannies in which sparrows can build their homes. Another is the shortage of insect food on which sparrows feed their chicks, and yet another is the inexorable rise in air pollution from motor vehicles – a particular problem for such a sedentary species. Finally, as is the case with so many birds of the countryside, there is the issue of modern farming practices. In the past, plenty of grain was left on the fields after harvest, or sparrows and other birds could feed in and around barns. Today, farms are far more careful, so spilled and waste seed and grain are virtually non-existent.

For the house martins, which migrate elsewhere instead of staying put like the sparrows, things have not worked out well either. During that same period, Britain has lost two out of three of its breeding house martins. The huge fall in the numbers of flying insects, combined with the disappearance of ponds and pools where the birds used to pick up the mud they need to build their nests, is undoubtedly to blame. And for these and many other species that migrate all the way to sub-Saharan Africa, from the whinchat to the wheatear and the spotted flycatcher to the swift, habitat loss across that vast continent has also led to major – and, for some, potentially irreversible – decline.

By far the biggest issue facing both resident and migratory wildlife is, without question, global climate change. I first became aware of its potential effects on birds back in the early 1990s, when I wrote my first book, *Birds and Weather*. I can still recall my dawning understanding as I realised that this was of a quite different category to any other threat.

Ironically, many regions of the world are already witnessing some of the local benefits of climate change. The arrival of new species from the European continent – including bee-eaters, great white egrets, and a host of moths and damselflies – is very exciting for those of us who live in southern England. We conveniently forget that in the north of Britain, that same climate change is promoting the rapid retreat of some of our most valued birds, such as the puffin, ptarmigan and snow bunting. As always, we tend to focus on what is happening on our home patch, which masks our awareness of the bigger picture.

That's where the migrants can help. By definition, these creatures are both local and global. They are born and raised alongside us – in the case of the house martin, literally so – and yet they travel greater distances in a year than most human beings do in a lifetime. So we need to start to see the world from their perspective, breaking down the borders between nations and cultures, and working together to solve these problems on a global scale.

And so, as I hear the call of the cuckoo over my local patch on a bright May morning, watch the house martins gliding above my village, or marvel at a hummingbird hawk-moth as it zooms around my garden, I pray that we will find a way to forestall these threats to our resident and migrant wildlife. For they provide an invisible thread that connects my own home with many millions of people I have never met, far away from here, who share a profound and lifelong love of the natural world. 🐦

# LIVING LAVA

## SHAPING SACRED LAND

*Words:* Annie Worsley
*Photography:* Leigh Hilbert

We live on a dynamic, living planet, born of elemental fire, earth, water and air. Our continents ride upon oceans of molten rock, making journeys imperceptible to the human senses. Throughout the long arch of time since our planet was formed, they have sailed back and forth in a dance of unimaginable potency. Continental drift has enabled the evolution of life in our oceans and the emergence and disappearance of great dynasties on land. It has contributed to our changing climate and the formation of Earth's greatest geomorphological spectacles. Where tectonic plates meet or diverge, crustal force is expressed in earthquakes and as volcanoes, and if it were possible to watch Earth's story from the beginning, we would see a colourful and extraordinarily beautiful entity that shifts and changes as if alive.

For most of us, movements and exchanges of energy between components of the geosphere are invisible, but for many the interior mysteries of our planet are revealed from time to time. Along the margins of continents, where mountain ranges are uplifted or where tectonic plates are being pulled apart by unseen, subsurface currents, evidence of Earth's internal character and motion is revealed. Dramatic changes to the planet's structure occur where volcanism and tectonic movement are at their most violent – around the Ring of Fire, which encircles the Pacific Basin. Yet some of the most beautiful and gentle eruptions are found in the centre of the Pacific, amongst the islands of Hawai'i.

The US state of Hawai'i is a 1,500-mile-long archipelago of islands that are the summits of subsea volcanic mountains. They were formed as the Pacific oceanic plate moved slowly across a hot spot of upwelling magma, which it continues to do at a rate of approximately 30 miles every million years. The islands at the north-eastern end of the chain are the oldest and most quiescent, whilst in the southeast Hawai'i Island (Big Island), with the largest volcanoes (Mauna Loa and Kīlauea), is the youngest and most active.    ≫→

Both Mauna Loa and Kīlauea are shield volcanoes, a name derived from their relatively flat domed shape, rather like a warrior's shield that has been laid down on a battleground. They are formed from gentle but effusive eruptions of basaltic lava, which flows easily because it has low viscosity and thereby spreads out in all directions around the crater, forming the characteristic low-lying dome.

The landscapes of these volcanic islands are mellow and gentle, subdued into feminine roundness and curves by dint of the internal chemistry of lava flows and methods of formation, and yet they are filled with evidence of elemental fire and motion. They also have a long association with myths and legend, in particular with the capricious and emotional Pele, who is known in Hawai'i as the goddess of volcanoes. Descended from the Sky Father, Pele is also goddess of fire, lightning and wind and is known as 'she who shapes sacred land', which enshrines her vivacious and passionate creative nature in every corner of the Hawaiian landscape.

Basaltic lava generated by Pele within the cauldrons of Mauna Loa and Kīlauea spread out in contiguous and continuous layers and over time formed the island of Hawai'i. Many of the layers can be dated using a range of geo-technologies, which has allowed geologists to construct a detailed history of Pele's efforts. Large swathes of the volcanic deposits and lava flows that make up Hawai'i's gently undulating landscape are contorted into fantastic shapes by the fluid dynamics of molten material that is both viscous and energetic. Almost as soon as lava erupts, its surface cools and darkens – the red-hot interior flow continues onwards whilst the outer crust contorts and cools. Where lava emerges onto gentle slopes, it forms long ropes, ribbons or blankets collectively known as pahoehoe. When these flows reach the sea, they cool in a maelstrom of steam and light.

The lava shapes found on Hawai'i are organic and motile. They exude heat, scent, sound and colour. There are mounds and cushions, ship's hawsers and tumbled bed sheets, and great gouts of crimson Hadean magic. The overwhelming influence of Pele is everywhere. Over the last thirty years eruptions from Halema'uma'u, the main crater of Kīlauea in the Puna region swept across the gardens, woodlands and town of Kalapana, vaporising homes and burning roads. And in 2018 the rest of the Lower Puna area was completely devastated by a major eruption of lava, the most destructive flow in 200 years. Thirty five square kilometres of land and more than seven hundred homes were lost. As Pele's flows reached the sea they created new land and reshaped the coast in tumbles of rainbows, lightning, scorching steams and red rivers.

In this way, once again Pele birthed a living world of fire and light. Neither the darkness of night nor the Pacific's ocean waters could obliterate her organic heat or match the majesty of her creative powers. As the flows began to cool and people were able to look once more at Kalapana, all they could see was a landscape overlain by the spreading coiled and braided tresses of Pele, mother of the Hawaiian islands.

# NATURE RED

POEMS BY ZETTA BEAR

*Illustration:* Justine Osborne

SKIN

In the moment between thinking
I'll call, and calling
he comes to me.

          He uses old fashioned language
          *how can I serve thee mistress*
          although I'm not his mistress –
          he chooses to please me
          because it's beautiful.

The curve of him floating
above the heath after a hare
is more glorious than
any handsome man.

          He's both bow and arrow
          as sprung, as straight
          as pure in his design.

Sometimes he presses
his forehead to mine
and we imagine his thick pelt
lying against the inside of my skin.

## MERLE

I'll remember best her muscled rump
powering over a hill towards mischief.
However close she sleeps
against my back at night,
however tight she shadows me,
however fierce she guards the door
she will not promise to obey.

        Old as a medieval tapestry
        generations drive her like a spear onto her prey.
        Deer, rabbit, fox and hare fall in her silent course.
        Half feral, against all strangers and some friends
        she hauls me behind her into trouble and out again.

But once, in the aftermath of a disaster
after we had run, bloodied, from the scene
and I could not look at the others for rage
she licked each shaken member of the pack
from nose to neck, slowly, firmly, nose to neck
until we could be still again. Until we could be still.

TERRIER

live wire
spitfire
hit list
clenched fist

      bush whack,
      whip crack
      wild spark
      sky lark

flick knife
hard life
bee hive
high five

      warm bed
      hot head
      loose thread
      daily bread

snip snap
hand clap
my beloved
steel trap.

A journal of nature & story